dedication

*To me, for having the courage to
free my heart to help you do the same.*

a note from the author

here's to all the words i ever wanted to share with you that were stored in my heart, hidden and at the tip of my tongue with hopes to release them in a safe and comfortable space like here, on pages where i'd be confident to let go; on pages where i could be free and express my thoughts, ideas, and life experiences through the power of sharing words from my heart.

here's to all the words i ever wanted to invite you to read because i know you're experiencing life storms, loss, self-love issues, depression, and pain. but don't worry. you're not alone; the world is also struggling. so please sit down and make yourself at home in my space, in one of my favorite places to be creative, sassy, loud, and expressive. we're survivors, and i'm glad we connected. here's my heart. let it inspire yours.

love,
Kala

Words from the Heart

A collection of inspirational poetry and prose

2ND EDITION

Kala Jordan-Lindsey

Words from the Heart - 2nd Edition

Copyright © 2023 by Kala Jordan-Lindsey

Book formatting and cover design: www.bookclaw.com
Editor: Sana Abuleil
Photo credits: Flawless j photography

Books may be purchased in quantity and for special sales by contacting Kala Jordan-Lindsey at:
Write@kalajordanlindsey.com

For more information, contact:
Kala Jordan-Lindsey
Write@kalajordanlindsey.com
www.kalajordanlindsey.com

To schedule a consultation, email:
Write@kalajordanlindsey.com

i'm free.

words from the heart

Contents

a journey in my heart

in my head

i'm sitting above my voice—in my head
in a dark and secluded space
as i roam around each stage of my life
in a circle covered in skin and bones.
i'm in the wilderness—not where i should be
i'm somewhere in chaos, somewhere on this dark planet
where it's noisy like the sound of a rock band playing
somewhere hiding like being underground
where no one knows, but me and God.
i'm confused like a blind girl gone wild…without alcohol
and cigarettes
stinking up my entire body.

hello, i'm here—in my own body
but i can't hear anything and i'm certain no one can hear me
except the noise that's coming from within—in my brain
and it's telling me lies
my heart is weak—sound asleep like a newborn resting
after a bottle.

that's because i'm unconscious.

the chatter is getting louder
the more i become aware of this noise
in my body.

i'm walking (in my own head)
i'm an ordinary human-being, but i'm not myself.
i'm a balloon that's ready to burst
like a firecracker

i am ready to deliver like an expecting mother at forty
weeks.
however, i don't expect to be here any longer—i have some
faith.

i am within proximity to my heart
an exit door i desire to release my thoughts and feelings.
i have so much to say but when i speak
it's only me in the room with my Father.
i'm imprisoned.
trapped in my head
where i see my heart at a distance but i can't hear it.
my intuition is louder.
my flesh wants its way
but my heart desires direction.
i don't hear my Father because my desire for the world is
louder.
walking around my head gives me more pleasure than any-
thing else
but i still feel smothered and imprisoned
like an unhappy caged bird wanting freedom.

i am in captivity to my own environment—my head
which is apart of my body, but i'm lost in this body
of mine.
i don't know what it is.
am i losing it or is my mind playing tricks on me?

i am someone else inside of my temple (my body)
with black, slanted eyes.
i am gazing around the world with laughs and smiles
but i'm silent.
i'm going along with the flow of the wind
like the waves in the ocean

as i stand near the exit door—my heart.
but i'm afraid to leave this cell of my life.
i want to release.
i want to be me like the picture of freedom without having
burdens over my shoulders.
but i am still in the wilderness.
i'm tired of looking at my footprints and playing the same
old damn
song.
i'm screaming inside but no one hears me because i'm in
my head.
my heart is noisy but only God hears me.
He knows because my tongue is in the same position as it
was when i was a child.
it's in my mouth and hasn't said a word.

but the good thing is that i have hope that one day God will
give me the strength
to say something,
to embrace my tongue, my powerful voice
before it's too late,
before i bury everything i ever wanted to say in the ground
eventually my bones would disappear, but not my soul.

my voice was hidden behind bars, behind the skin and bones
my Father
created.

i'm standing outside my head.

i stood behind my bright, beautiful smile
and ran many miles
in my head
in a wilderness.

my circle wasn't large because my head overpowered my
heart.
i was imprisoned and i wanted to escape
the walls of fear and low self-esteem.
i never started a conversation but fear had my tongue.
so, i sat in my head and listened to others like listening to a
concert.

i wanted to share every letter that produced my story
but i couldn't.
i'm confident to say that today
i can finally smile
i'm black, humbled, and i'm proud.

as a teen i was asleep
spiritually weak
tired
like a football player's energy
after a game.

i walked a distance in the heat
while covering my eyes because i was afraid to rise
while rockin' and rollin' with none of God's sheep.
i held my head down to the beat and fell asleep
without a call or a beep
but reminiscing about when i was child
and how i ran many miles
with my bright and beautiful smile
it kept me encouraged.
but honey child
i'm confident to say that today
i can finally smile.
i'm black, humbled, and i'm proud

as a woman i walked down aisles
and hid my bold smiles
through all my trials
and didn't know who to dial
so, i hid my habits, thoughts
and words from the heart behind the scenes
with my other dreams
in my sexy and blue skinny jeans
thinking i'd never be seen.
but Lord knows i had so much to say
but i was uncertain
as i sat behind the curtains.
but honey child
i'm confident to say that today
i can finally smile.
i'm black and i'm proud.

today, i'm stepping up and stepping out
because God blessed me with this choice
to no longer be afraid
to share my impactful voice
with my beautiful, brown-skinned glow.
i'm not writing to boast.
my confidence is in what God certainly knows
in my identity, which is now exposed.

but today, i'm no longer hiding in the clouds
i'm black, humbled, and i'm proud
with my sweet, brown, and imperfect skin
that has also sinned
but my eyes are opened today.
i have faith that i'll continue to win
with my visible voice.
i thank God for blessing me to make the choice.
i sit, smile, and rejoice

while thanking God for revealing His amazing voice.
i'm black, humbled, and i'm proud.

i'm confident in my skin.

a painting of my heart

it's quiet and i'm standing in the middle of a familiar place
where there are no other humans except me
because i'm here in my own body.
i'm in proximity to my heart—i'm in the middle of my chest
near the beauty mark above my breast
below my beautiful face
where it's quiet except for the sound of my heartbeat.

i'm walking around my heart
like a person viewing a painting on a wall—except i'm not
in a museum
somewhere on earth.
i'm in a temple surrounded by organs—my own—scarred as
hell.
i see the shadow of my precious body past every part man
judges
and verbally attacks.
i'm deeper than my skin and bones—the fragile parts God
created
in my mother's womb.

the outside of my body is covered in brown
with scars buried deep within my heart.

here's a painting of my heart:

it's big and creative like the rainbow
except smaller than my body.

it's expressive like my hands
noisy when it's anxious

and rejoices in the Lord.

it's beautiful like my eyes
loves unconditionally
gives and forgives
and treats others with compassion.

it's round like a circle, but imperfect because i'm human.

i welcome you to sit with me in my heart
on the left side of my upper body near my chest.

you're welcome to stare
but don't judge me.
when you see me, look through my eyes
not at my eyes
look through my face
not at my face
look through my hair
not at my hair
look through my clothes
not at my clothes
look through my moves
not at my moves
look through my eyes
not at my eyes
look through my heart
not at my heart
listen
listen
listen
listen through my voice
not at my voice.

here's a picture of my heart like a painting on the wall.

we're all unique and precious. embrace your heart.

inspiration

yes

yes
creates opportunity
to say yes
is the opportunity
yes
is the opposite of "unfortunately, no"
to say yes
is the opposite of no
yes
is the light at the end of the tunnel
to say yes
gives a chance
yes
touches the heart
to say yes
encourages
inspires
and motivates.

recycle your no's and let them inspire you until you get a yes.

confidence

the color of my skin

the color of my skin is just a pigment covering my bones.
it doesn't define who i am because my identity is found
in Jesus Christ, the One who created my insides and every-
thing you see
on the outside like the color of my skin.

it's the opposite of white
i'm not black like the dirt you spit on when you're uncon-
scious or having fun
nor am i a nigga like the one you read about in the dictio-
nary.
these are just words, not my identity
so, call me what you know—not what you desire to see
like the perfect image in your brains.
i'm nowhere near perfection because it doesn't define
the color of my skin.

i'm a woman, a human being designed with
the most powerful hands ever.
i'm a person with brown skin
like the color of wood.

i'm strong
fragile
and more powerful than you think.
i'm beautiful just the way i am
in this skin.

the color of my skin.
it's unique

not created to overpower
rule
seek evil
and fight with weapons.

God's word is my protection.

we were created winners.

life is not about our skin
but why does it offend your heart?
we fuss and fight
we debate
and choose light over dark.

we're both smart.

all lives matter

we're phenomenal
and intelligent
it's in our skin.

the color of my skin is beautiful
with flaws
beauty marks
and scars
on my neck
back
chin
over my temple
and within.

embrace it

stay confident
you're blessed beyond
the color of your skin

yes
i'm in love with the color of my skin.
it's a part of the rainbow and blessed
on purpose.
it's caramel
smooth
and vibrant.
i'm more valuable than the color of
my skin.

the color of my skin is not who i am within.

brown lips

i am a part of my body and settled on my face
i'm like a magnet; i'm in sync with my skin
i love my brown lips.

look above my cheeks
where my eyes can be seen moving left to right and up and
down.
i am down the street from my ears and at a distance from my
forehead.
no wonder you can spot me; i'm exposed.

can you see me?

i'm in front of you, before your precious eyes.

i'm round and designed with a perfect curve
like my behind—i'm always noticed without anything extra.
i'm beautiful and wonderfully made.

i don't need extra hands hovering over my face with instru-
ments
like screws and other silver things that enhance what
God created.

honey, i'm natural just the way i am
and when i'm at rest
my brown lips are eye-catching and gives my lover goose-
bumps
like the butterflies i get when he kisses me
on my neck, chest, and soft, beautiful lips.

i love the dip at the center of my top lip

where my lover joins his brown lips with mine.
we joined at the beach and looked out in the ocean
as we embraced the cool breeze.
then we looked at each other in the eyes and kissed
as the stars lit the sky.

he acknowledges that my brown lips are sweet like honey
and unique.
they're his
and his are mine because we're one.

my lips are loved and treated with special care.
i'm a diamond and adored like the stars in the sky.
i was discovered like the Greatest in the world.
i am embraced and treated like a queen with dignity
and honor.
i am loved and handled with caution
like a newborn.

i was created by my Father
to speak words of love and kindness.
i was designed to glorify my Father and praise His name.

i love my gifts.
i'm grateful and overjoyed.
i'm in love with my brown lips.

embrace yours and smile.

love your lips.

lost

i didn't know my name

for years i walked in my own body.
i am disconnected with my Father like a blind man
without direction.
i'm unconscious with anesthesia
totally lost.
it's strange because i heard a heartbeat, but i couldn't hear
mine
i was clueless
and blind.
i didn't know my name.

i'm laying under a white comforter and colored sheets
where his touch gives me butterflies.
i'm in heaven when he shifts me from left to right
and i face his luxurious headboard.
having orgasm after orgasm makes me feel loved.
but after the performance, i feel worthless.
i'm in pain as if i was physically bruised and given a thorn
in my heart.
i didn't know my name.

my brains went in circles
like the picture of a lollipop
i live in this circle
where darkness and heat are my environment.
my atmosphere is earth, but i'm still lost
and i'm dehydrated in hell.
i'm malnourished because i'm disconnected with my Father.
i'm walking in spiritual darkness
where my body is not getting what it needs.
it's deteriorating like a dead person in the grave.

i desire Living Water, but i'm clueless.
i'm naïve and i want to see.
i didn't know my name.

i'm ashamed and embarrassed because i only know
the direction of my left and right hand like a child.
i'm not ignorant; i can read, but i don't understand the Man-
ual of life.
i didn't know my name.

i'm young but he's older and he's playing these same old
games.

he tricks me like checkers with his intelligence
but i'm starting to read his mind
and the games he's playing.

i didn't know who to blame
for years i was clueless
but God released the chain.
i tried to depart this burden
for twelve years.
i jumped over hurdles
every day and weekend were the same
sex and love making was no different.
i lied down in chains.
i wanted to escape this wilderness.
i was in pain.
tears dripped from my eyes like rain.
you know me but not my name.

i was young and naïve
can you believe it?
my vision was black
as i gazed at text messages.
you may know me
but not my name.

i was left in the rain
cold
and heat.
i expected to be rescued.

i was in pain
but God came to release my shame.
i thought i was deep in love
but God said, "No, look way above."
His name is Love.
you know me but not my name.

you're more precious and valuable than your name.

affirmation

i'm beautiful just the way i am

every time i look in the mirror
it opposes me with a "do not enter" voice that's coming
from my heart
and it's driving me nuts like the sound of a prisoner shouting
for freedom.
it's strange because the prisoner is me and i'm trying to
escape
but i can't—can somebody help me?
why do i poke dents in my cheeks with my fingers to make
dimples?
i see others with them and it makes them look beautiful so i
want a pair.
i think if i had them, others would treat me different but
most of all,
i'll be content like a child who gets her way.

the hard part about this routine is that i'm tired of feeling
disconnected
i feel left out because i don't have dimples.
it looks like i've never slept with bags underneath my eyes.
is this normal? am i still beautiful or what?

well, i'm talking to myself because it's just me—
no one else is around in this mirror nor in my head.
i feel alone like an isolated human being.
i want to socialize, too, but i'm shy and have low self-es-
teem.
i also stutter, so how am i suppose to feel beautiful or am i
beautiful?

i've walked here for years, but nothing hasn't changed—

how long will this last?

i'm used to my environment—bathroom mirrors that oppose
my image because i'm not satisfied in this skin.
so i'm standing far away from the mirror.
every day i face this haunting spot my stomach aches
like the scene of watching a woman vomit for years.
what an uncomfortable scene and one i never imagined.
but not only that
i hate turning on the light because i haven't learned to em-
brace the dimness
and imperfections of my body—the one my Father created.
so now it's the place i like to visit least
but there's no way for me to stop.
i must use the restroom to release this stuff out of my body
and clean these germs off
but most of all, to finally face my fear.

so now i'm smiling after all these years.

i'm confident and realize i'm beautiful just the way i am.
dimples and the perfect eyes don't define my beauty.
i was created and wonderfully made by a perfect God
who designed me without any mistake.

when you see me, it's not a fluke like the ones i make in this
skin.
i'm authentic.
i'm beautiful just the way i am
like the butterflies God created to fly.
and cover girl—it doesn't define me—i don't need makeup
to cover what i don't want others to see.
i'm okay and have no shame in wearing skinny jeans.

i'm beautiful without Revlon to cover my scars
or mac to hide the blemishes of my life.
i'm beautiful in skinny jeans
you're beautiful without Burberry
you're beautiful without Coach
you're beautiful without Michael Kors
you're beautiful just the way you are
you're beautiful because you were carefully knitted in your
mother's womb
you're beautiful
you're beautiful because God loved you enough that He
created you
you're beautiful
you're beautiful because God created you on purpose, with
purpose, and for a
greater purpose
you're beautiful just the way you are
you're beautiful without the extras, glamour, and glow
you're beautiful just the way you are
without the *bling bling* and diamond rings
you're beautiful just the way you are
just keep walking, pray, and keep your eyes focused the
other way
life is too short
if you're tempted, just check into a resort
walk boldly, courageously, confidently, and with faith any-
way.
don't worry about what people say
because you're beautiful in every way.

you're beautiful naked.

naive

young

i'm young and naïve
and i don't understand life because i'm blind like a person
who can't see
so i don't know which way to go or whether left or right is
the right choice
but i'm sure i'll figure it out—if figuring it out is based on
my own intuition.

i'm an inexperienced black girl with hopes and dreams and
right now
i want to explore life—i want to try new things to see how it
feels
everybody else is doing it so i wanna try too
as i walk with my mouth closed but heart sticking out my
chest to just be human—to explore me and others.

i'm on this road and i'm experiencing obstacles.
i'm struggling with life because i'm trying to figure it out
without the One who is the truth, way, and life—God
but i'm young and i really don't know—i don't understand
how to live a disciplined life—my environment is dysfunc-
tional and i know this
because i speak to my dad but he's not in the same house—
he's somewhere up the road.
my mom is struggling in this house.
she's struggling to pay bills and put food on the table
so she's doing any and everything she can to help take care
of my sisters and i.
it's difficult, but God is making a way out of no way.
my daddy helps—when he can.
my sisters and i kind of understand but not fully.

we love our parents despite the separation in this house.
my mom worked hard and sacrificed her time and freedom
for my sisters and i.
we love daddy and mama, but we don't understand why he's
not with mama.
well, years later we did, but now daddy just had a stroke,
and we think he's about to die, but he doesn't—thank God.

life is different now because my daddy doesn't function the
same.
he's in a wheelchair and his left arm doesn't work
like it did before he laid in this nursing home.
but he's improving, each day—he's getting stronger as we
stop near the cemetery
and visit him.
we're just a few minutes away so we stop over and support
our daddy.
he's smiling and telling everyone about this brain stroke he
had.
He's praising God as well—the One who saved his life to
give up his life for His sake.
we love him and thank God for him.

so, months have passed and now daddy is walking
except with a limp and his right hand doesn't function how
it did years ago.
daddy is preparing to live in a nursing facility but my sisters
and i are kind of home alone—temporary while my mother
serves times up north for the love of my sisters and i—what
a difficult situation.
but we know one day mommy will be home—we can't wait
so we write her letters and talk to her on the phone.
she loves hearing our voices and we love reading her incom-
ing letters.

i guess one day i'll get it and understand why i feel this way
and why life is as it is.

my oldest sister and i are driving up to visit mommy.
what a long drive, but we love seeing the mountains—i nev-
er saw this environment.
we're here and it looks like a university campus with dorms
and i'm struggling while walking up these hills
but it's okay because now i see mommy!
she hugged us and gave us kisses with her beautiful smile.
she looked healthy and strong—where she was that was the
only way to survive
she prayed and stayed strong.
she'll be home soon.

yay! mommy is now home, and we can breathe.
we're excited and thank God for delivering her safe and
sound
to the doorstep where my heart resided.

it's not over until i understand what it means to mature.

i'm mature—i'm no longer that young, black girl
who was clueless about my surroundings.
i thank God for His grace.
i never had a reason to hold my thumb out at a distance from
my temple
yelling, "here i am"
lay on me and come.
i loved to have fun and i loved to run in the sun.
i watched my tongue
though i was sprung.
i was just young
i didn't care for late night fun

past the rising sun
nor did i stand out
asking men to sleep with me
walking the streets
just to lay under the sheets.
i was just naïve
spiritually blinded
and lost.
but what's amazing
and mind blowing
is that
i was protected by the One
and only Son.
i was young
that's why i let him cum
it was a hard run
because i had so much fun
but it's sad
because i cried under the authority of
the magnificent Son.
i was young
i never realized what i had done.

i was young.
i wasn't perfect
nor were you.
we've all sinned and ran astray
from the Son.
i'm thankful
because God forgives.
remember
He first loved us
amid our sins.
i knew one day

i would escape
like the fast and the furious.

i was a teen
lost and clueless
but now…
i thank God.
He continues to renew my mindset
His grace and mercy saved my life
i can breathe

i'm free at last
thank God, Almighty
i'm free.

i have an intimate relationship with Jesus Christ
the One true Son.

my past is an old, yet powerful, inspirational song.

loss

miss you

i'm entering the building and i'm scared as hell.
i'm nervous and i don't know what the heck to do.
am i crazy or not or is this normal?
i'm somewhere i don't wanna be.
i'm embarrassed and feel like giving up.
who can i call?
can anybody hear my heart?
it's bleeding with another precious human being inside.
i'm young and confused about life
and feel brain washed.
i feel like i've been raped and spit on
but now it seems too late because i'm here now.
it feels like i'm walking in a tunnel without the Light.
i walk to the back of this place and lay down on an unusual
bed
like i've lost my mind when minutes later i awake and look
around
like a lost child
i'm speechless
but Lord knows i miss you, baby
more than words could ever express
i think of you more
not less
because you were a part of my flesh
i know you're in Heaven
looking down in peace and at rest
i love you.

i miss you, baby
more than anyone would ever understand
my heart is filled with words like a swollen gland.
Lord knows i think about you every day and at every chance

i wish i could hold you, today, in my precious, brown hands
i love you.

i miss you, baby.
some days are still tough
yes, it gets a little rough
like the texture of the hardest chocolate chip cookie dough
only God knows
i love you.

i miss you, baby
you will always be mine
a precious, one of a kind
who will always shine
you are mine
Lord knows
if only i could turn back the hands of time
you would be in my arms.
i love you
and i miss you, baby.

you'll forever be my angel.

in this skin

my pretty tone skin

it's me again
except with a different attitude.
i'm confident—bold and sassy unapologetically.
i love me and my pretty tone skin like never before.

i adore how it looks and feels like the sight and touch of his
warm body
against mine—what a beautiful scene as i watch my pretty
tone skin
unite with his and we embrace each other.

i'm strong and unmovable like a house built on a firm foun-
dation
and like a tree planted in the ground.
i feel good about myself—my self-esteem is no longer at the
bottom of the sea.

i love me and my pretty tone skin.
it's smooth like buttercream and unbreakable like my heart.
i'm in love with my pretty tone skin.

i love me.

don't lose your mind

i am far away from my body like a wandering child, who's
lost in the woods.
my brain is disconnected from me, and i'm clueless.
i'm detached from where my heart beats, which is strange.
it's uncomfortable walking on earth without a clear con-
scious.
it's hard like a rock—i hope this never happens again…

hello—can you hear me or am i alone in this?
is anyone else experiencing this scary, dark side of life
where you're attached
from your head like a blind man without purpose?
have i really lost my mind or what?
i'm in the middle of somewhere trying to get my head to-
gether like my life,
but i've lost my mind—i'm shouting for help,
but i'm not sure if anyone hears me…God does,
but can anyone else hear me
if i'm silent with a precious voice bloated with so much to
say?

wow, i guess this is my reality.
i never expected to lose my mind from such a pretty body as
mine.
i'm the perfect size and shape with the most beautiful eyes
on the planet—
well, that's what they all say and more.
i have indian hair and the coolest bob in the world.
my clothes are clean and i'm not ignorant—i talk with sense
with my sexy voice.
but wait, that's not all.
i also have two degrees so i'm certified to teach your child

music
but now it's hard for me to get a job....
is it true that if you've emptied your pockets
and live on debt that you'll get the perfect job
to make enough money to pay every bill that comes through
the mailbox?

i guess it's strange because i've lost my mind
without ever being on drugs and alcohol like the black and
mild
cigarettes and corona i smell breezing through the vents in
my apartment.
this stinks and i pity my daughter shouting "mama, what is
that smell,
why does it smell in here?"
i guess this is the experience of living in the hood or ghetto
or whatever
you call it—but it's okay because better days are here and
better days are coming.

right now, i'm more thankful than ever
because i once was lost but now i'm found.
my mind is now in proximity to my heart—we've reunited
like a married couple, after years of separation.

i'm in my right mind, to God be the glory.
yay!
i'm so thankful
i can jump up and shout a million times like a child on their
birthday.

i'm overjoyed because it was only by the grace and mercy
of God
that He delivered me from darkness to light

from the wilderness to His presence.
He put me back together like a broken heart.
i'm walking with the Lord
and i'm confident my life is in harmony with His word.

so, embrace your brain—the one you're using now.
don't lose your mind
or else's you'll be blind.

the Good News is here, so sit up and listen up.
read and study the Word.
and don't take life for granted.
be wise so you don't fall behind like a trampling animal.
tell the truth like the opposite of a myth.
do your best and be sure to rest—take care of your body and
don't lose
your mind.

be conscious because you need it like every breath you take.

i'm praying you never lose your mind because it's precious
beyond silver and gold and all the riches in the world.
it has the power to save you or destroy your soul.

don't lose your mind—embrace it.
nourish it like never before.
how? well, feed it with the Word.
desire to do good.
be kind.
bless others.
love your neighbor
have respect
and never give up.
walk with open eyes

and embrace it unlike your possessions.
own it and never neglect it.
don't neglect it like trash—it's more valuable than garbage.
don't lose your mind.
love it.

never lose your mind.

songs of praise

but God

as i reflect on chapters of my
life
each one is sure to have the
presence of God
because if it had not been for
Him
i'd still be lost or in my grave
watching my bones crumble
from heaven.
but God...

i couldn't see so i craved the
things of this world and al-
most crashed, but God...
i was young, naïve, and clue-
less about life
so, i was a follower, not a
leader, until i surrounded
myself around loved ones,
friends and family
that encouraged me and
taught me about the Truth,
Way, and Life—my God.

i didn't listen because i desired
the noise of life over God's
voice.
so, discipline was just a word on
my vocabulary list
i didn't take life seriously, but
God...
i was disobedient so it was hard
to shine my light.
darkness overpowered my
thoughts and actions like alcohol
that overpowers a drunken man.

i struggled with life since i was born like the man with lep-
rosy
and the woman who bled.
i ran around the same circle and bumped my head.
sometimes it hurt and sometimes it didn't.
i was used to these obstacles like listening to the same old
damn song.
i was tired, but my heart wasn't because i continued to
grind.
crazy, right? well, it's the truth.
but God…

living in poverty and around
others who had less was real—it
wasn't a game like *mario*
i dearly loved when i was a child.
day and night were the same
it was a struggle to live—com-
fortably—in the days and after.
boy oh boy, i hate seeing my
pockets empty.
i was broke, but not broken.
i had no money because i didn't know what to do with it.
so, loans were my first choice than gaining green this way.
i wanted it fast—to work was more, which led me to experi-
ence
seasons of unemployment.
but God made a way out of no way as i hit rock bottom
and almost lost every part in my body
like my mind when i want to quit and give up on everything
in front of me including my heart.
but God kept me and blessed me to overcome depression
when i lost everything
i gained from the world
except my heart, mind, and soul.

so now i praise His holy name because
grace and mercy restored me without the strength of man
but God who continues to renew my mindset when i rise.

the power of grace allows you to taste a "but God" experi-
ence.

the Lord is my song

He's my Song
i have a testimony to sing
He's my Song
i have a story to sing
He's my Song
His glory made me sing
He's my Song
His love, blood, grace, and mercy made me sing
He's my Song
my trials and tribulations made me sing
He's my Song
my struggles made me sing
He's my Song
my obstacles made me sing
He's my Song
my hills and tunnels made me sing
He's my Song
my mountains made me sing
He's my Song
my deepest valleys made me sing
He's my Song
His powerful grace made me sing
He's my Song
my toughest nights made me sing
He's my Song
my smiles made me sing
He's my Song
my sleepless nights made me sing
He's my Song
my days my days, oh my, i sang
He's my Song
my *yes* and *no's* made me sing

it wasn't man but the Man above, made me sing

He's my Song
my happy days made me sing
He's my Song
that man made me sing
He's my Song
oh, my God made me sing
He's my Song.

embrace my Song.

dreams to calling

dreams

i was that girl with short legs
like an unbroken broom
near my mother's room.
i stood tall
like an unwavering tree.
i rose like a soldier
with confidence
and excitement.
i had dreams.
i wanted to shoot threes
because basketball was my favorite sport.
i wanted to play in the WNBA.
i wanted to be everything.
i had dreams
when i was a child.
i laughed
joked
and smiled.

like a child that sleeps
slumbers
and snores only to be awakened
with excitement
joy
laughter
smiles
her eyes years later
only to realize it was just a dream.
her calling was deeper.

i had dreams
that made me think about

the experience
of tasting that delicious ice cream.
i had dreams to become a brain
and heart surgeon
to become a chiropractor
to become an FBI agent
or to play in the top orchestra
in the world.
i had dreams
unlike what God created me to be.
but now i realize
my calling is more powerful than
my dreams.

your calling is more powerful than your dreams.

hardships

i didn't have a dime

my pockets were empty.
i didn't have a dime
so, i had to use my mind
i didn't want to waste time.
i continued to grind
thanks to the Holy Spirit
for each day, guiding what was on my mind
so my voice would shine, oh yes!

He said, "you are ever special"
and He renewed my mind
so i could help and encourage the blind.
i didn't have a dime
but He gave me the confidence i needed to shine
to renew my mind and write these rhymes
and inspirational messages.
i write all the time.
i had a choice.
so, i used my voice
and started writing.
i have no remorse.
i was motivated to take advantage of my time
so that, one day, i wouldn't have to continue the grind.
i didn't have a dime
but now i'm rich
in my Father.
i'm blessed and continue to shine.

i was broke, not broken.

my inner voice .

i'm invisible because i'm hiding somewhere in my body
and i can't get out.
i'm trapped in my heart but i can't be heard because i'm
roaming
like a lost child except i'm older now
and it's still hard for me to get out—to say something.
my heart is loud but i'm stuck in silence.
i'm in an empty room where no one can hear me
except myself, and i feel lonely
but i have hope that one day i'll release
my voice where it feels like someone is holding my tongue
like a person bending a rubber band without releasing it.

help
somebody, please help me
i wanna get out of here but i just don't know how...
i have so much to share with you but i can't
until i'm confident enough to let go of my fears and con-
cerns.
i feel like the earth is on my head
spinning without my voice
without me—what's going on?
why do i hear myself in my own body but the world
doesn't?
i guess i'll push like a pregnant woman giving birth
until it's delivered from my favorite spot to hang out.

yes!
i can feel it
i'm getting stronger, each day
and i'm more confident than ever
because i'm certain someone hears me inside of here.
someone knows i'm trapped in my own body and they're
praying
they're encouraging me and motivating me to keep going
to keep pushing and rising above my obstacles
in this small but powerful little world i'm in.

for years i hovered around a heart that was anxious about
escaping its body
because it had so much to say that it was expected
to explode on any day now
like an inexperienced girl waiting to have her first orgasm
out of this world
with butterflies exciting her hormones until the hour finally
arrives
like the sunrise in the morning and countdown to the new
year.
five, four, three, two, one—i'm free now
my inner voice rejoices like a heart that's renewed
and nourished by the Spirit.
it's out of my heart where it once settled
it sings.
i am thankful for my inner voice
it's a blessing and gift—
one i'll always embrace.

every day i use it because it's my choice.
i have confidence—
it's stored in my heart
deep down in my soul.
i feel good.
i could have given my worship in Christ a divorce
but, to speak through my amazing
beautiful voice is a blessing.
i rejoice because He's my
hunger
not the world no longer.
i thank God in my weakness
because then i am strong.

i love to speak

i will always teach when i stand on my feet
not just at the beach.
God blessed me with the passion to inspire hearts in homes
schools
communities
and in these streets
so, i'm thankful
oh, yes!
let the world hear your beautiful voice.

embrace your voice.

unforgettable

it was quiet
like the sound of an empty bedroom
but my heart was noisy like a crying baby.
i was uncomfortable and anxious like a person with a heavy
heart.
my heart is flooding with the stresses and tension of life
and i'm nervous—i want this day and season of my life to
pass
as fast as the wind as if i never experienced it.
i'm shaky and tears are flooding my brains like i wanna
explode—
all in one body…. the atmosphere is unforgettable.
i'm not use to it as i gaze at familiar and unfamiliar faces
like strangers and friends.

this is odd and not what i expected—something unforgetta-
ble.

it's making me nervous and upset every time i hear these
familiar voices
attached to uncompassionate hearts—like really….
is this real or not? am i dreaming or is this my reality?

my heart can't take it anymore—i'm pregnant with words
that what i wanna say i can't so i'm walking by faith.
i'm letting the Spirit guide my thoughts before i release my
tongue.
i'm loaded with so much on my heart like a balloon getting
ready to burst.

i was filled with words from the heart
and memories where seconds turned into minutes

that reflected on unforgettable moments
school days
holidays
performances
laughs
smiles
arguments
and when the ordinary turned into the unexpected
day
like the visual of peace and chaos.

my head spun
like an uncontrollable tornado
without a land.

there was tension
when i sat down
only to listen to hearts filled with lies.

i cried
in my own pool of tears
like a never-ending river.

i was locked in a room
smothered
caged in
and humiliated.

i felt my head turning like a milkshake
imprisoned in hell
like a cage bird yelling for freedom.

i was tired
drained

upset
and craved peace.

what an hour of…

i thank God for keeping me strong.
His grace and mercy covered me
with His right arm.

my life was unexpectedly touched.
what an unforgettable moment
day
season
and year.

the unforgettable things of life are a part of my true story.

deliverance

rescued

for years
i walked in a wilderness
like a child who wandered in a maze
without following a map, the Manual of Life.
i didn't know whether to turn
left or right.
i ran straight into the real world
like jumping into a pool
and drowning.
my life was complicated.
and i lost my mind.
so, i continued in a valley.
it was dark like the storms of life
gray and black
with very few rainbows.
i was lost
spiritually naked
malnourished
and blind.

i didn't understand
so, i bumped my head.
life was a game
like the nintendo i played.
sometimes i won
and some days i lost.
i felt like a failure
broke without a dime.

i lost my mind
like a scattered puzzle.
i was confused
and walked in the wilderness.

i sang the same song
until the Lord rescued me

out of my afflictions
storms
battles
chaos
trauma
depression
and temple.

He rescued me
from the wilderness
like the Father
who recues His children
from the deaths of life.

so, the first time it happened…
when i rose
i released—it felt like i was in heaven.
it was an experience that invited me into

such an atmosphere and environment
that i never considered
until i released the fear
shame
and embarrassment out of me
by unclogging my unhealthy
heart full of hurt and pain

joy and excitement
encouragement and inspiration
stories and testimonies
and praise to God until i finally realized
my heart was healthy.

my mindset was renewed
and i was experiencing freedom in Christ
a taste more powerful and valuable
than the richest man in the world
i experienced confirmation of my calling

my passion.

i was rescued
thank God, Almighty
i'm free at last.

He was there the entire time.

He slowed me down

i am young and naïve like a child riding a tricycle with
training wheels.
i am inexperienced without a clue about life and which way
to go.
if you ask me, i don't know—i'm still growing and learning
on this race of life as i run in the fast lane.

no wonder i have energy like an athlete
my life is going faster than light because i'm speeding.
now everything is falling apart and it's running me to the
ground.
and i'm drained like after having a long day in the sun
but God slowed me down to my knees
He allowed me to taste life until it pierced my life
like a painful thorn that i experienced down the road.

my heartbeat is fast, and my body is running around town
like a wild animal without discipline.

He slowed me down
like walking in a circle in the wilderness
around town.
God rescued me to where i could be found.

He slowed me down
so now i'm thankful that i can finally hear every heartbeat.
i once was lost but now i'm found.

He slowed me down
now i bend my knees to the ground
i thank the Lord, i was found

uh, how i love that He slowed me down.
i'm thankful because
He slowed me down.

the Lord slowed me down, and i'm thankful.

i know

i have the biggest smile on my face
like a person whose eyes are open after years of being blind
without a diagnosis.
so, i know how it is to be happy—to finally breathe—to be
human
because i didn't know how to exhale this stuff
like scrambled letters that were words to my story.
i didn't know how to just be like ordinary people you see
on the sidewalk and at the beach yelling and screaming
their lungs out to just be happy and enjoy life while the
lights are on
while the sun is shining, and the earth is spinning.
i am happy and nothing less.

i'm confident because my heart and mind are united
they're functioning the right way and no other way.
so i'm pleased and my Father is—and this i know because i
have faith.
i'm living rather than just being a participant of life like a
person
performing the daily routines of life—from sunrise to sunset
and then again—the way of life—inhaling and exhaling
like what you're doing now.
i am free without chains on my heart—it's beating normal
i can hear my heartbeat unlike since the day i was born.
i'm breathing after years of seeking life with a veil over my
eyes.
spiritual darkness covered my entire body—it poisoned my
organs
and sight—this i know—it's the truth.

yay!

i'm rejoicing today because i'm fulfilled
i'm a new person designed by the same God
who created me before i was born
this is my identity—the real one, not the one years ago.
i can sing without being afraid or doubtful because i know
how it is
to overcome life in the right One, in Jesus Christ.
this i know.

i'm stronger than yesterday and wiser than i've ever been.

i know how it is to experience trials and tribulations, and
trauma
it's painful to taste unlike a glass of sweet wine—it's re-
freshing
but watching a loved one die in your sleep is not.
my heart was torn, it was weak and hurt because the impact
hit hard
i was sad and out of it—lost because i didn't know how
long healing lasted
until i realized healing is a lifetime process
not a piece of cake like many portray trauma to be.
and this i know.

i know how it is to be rejected
by society like useless trash—like a human being
crumbled and kicked to the curve
thrown in a parking lot
and into the streets
with smiles and laughs
with goodbyes and see ya later.

i also know how it is to be adored by a neighbor—

by society like a fan that's loved.

i know how it is to live single—alone without a helpmeet
but i also know how it is to be happily married to the man
unlike the one in my dreams.
he's the one i prayed for when i was lost in the wilderness
when i shed tears in a bucket for someone to love me
instead of my body—the one and only one i have.
this i know.

but now i'm hurting—this year i lost my best friend to can-
cer
and it sucks.
she was beautiful.
we smiled, laughed, and drove around town—and away
from the usual.
we took everything with us including our own luggage—the
good and the bad
and the happy and sad like the stuff we coped with.

i know how it is to lose a loved one, but also how it is to live
in poverty
and around many who had less or nothing except a smile
and loving heart.
wealth was rarely discussed in my household because we
just didn't have it
we lived far away from those who had it "all."
it was hard and watching my mother struggle
was emotionally difficult more than ever like watching a
loved one
start from the bottom and sweat to rise and make it to the
top.

i know how it is to obtain health insurance—it's tough like

dough.

it's uncomfortable being told *yes* and *no* and sometimes
sitting in silence.
i know how it is to be treated equally and unequally
like a slave or a human with a different skin pigment.

i know how it is to be lied to
and to hear honesty—the truth.

i know how it is to be of the world.
i know how it is to be a child of God.

embrace both sides of the fence.

perseverance

the mountains, we climb

from sunrise to sunset
the earth spins and life goes on
like a clock—it's endless
like the mountains, we climb—each day
until death do us part.

when the birds chirp and roosters crow
the sun rises like a beautiful butterfly—
it stands like an immovable soldier
like you and i
with confidence…. ready to fight
to persevere
and overcome life
like the mountains, we climb.

we were born to fly—to rise beyond darkness—not to sleep
but to awake to grace and appreciate better days—
now and forever, so expect to win
as you swim through the waters
of life—the uncontrollable things out of your hands
the unexpectedness waiting at your door.

look up and strive each day with faith
and boldness as you climb
each day—every second, every minute of life
with open eyes as far as to the north
east, south, and west.

your remarkable resilience never stops.
it inspires lives.
so stand strong with hope like never before
and lean forward—not back
when you slip and fall—when you fail
and lose sight of your goals—look up
where the stars and the moon settle like the rainbow
after the storm.
you can do it because you were built with strength
and power to make it—to cross over stumbling blocks of
difficulties—

you were created to succeed the mountains, we climb.

hold your head up—high like the sky—yes, stand up ready
for battle—the obstacles of life—the tribulations of this
world—everything will be alright
as you move left to right
walk it out
kick, climb, and jump
higher as you look upon your deliverance
with every breath you take and every move you make.

be courageous and wise for the ones that refuse to endure
these mountains, we climb—pray—be compassionate, lov-
ing
and shine like the sun—bright yellow
unapologetically with a smile.

let's climb—we're stronger together.

climb and never give up.

faith

on this course of life
you will struggle
and face many trials and tribulations
like slaves who fought for freedom
on boats and fields
where blood, sweat, and tears
became scars of grace
and mercy.
so, don't be discouraged
and don't worry.
have faith—believe more than your
intuition.

you can do it.

you're an overcomer
a human being, who was created
on purpose, with purpose
and for a greater purpose
to walk by faith
and not by sight.

have faith
and rise like the morning sun.
you can do it, but God will make it hap-
pen.
so, believe in Him
and strive to do your best.
never give up.

you have what it takes
you're strong
brave
and courageous
so, be fearless
keep going
and encourage others along the way.

you're one of a kind.

have faith
it's a powerful choice
like never getting a divorce.
it's a gift with a purpose for your soul's sake
don't worry

because we all make mistakes
but God always paves a way
so, just sit down and pray.

walk by faith
when you get discouraged
and never doubt
the Lord loves unconditionally.

walk by faith
because He's better to us
that i can say

and always pray.
don't sway your faith the other way
stay focused
and stop worrying every day.
God works in mysterious ways
so, be quiet, always obey

and don't give up!
do as the Lord says
be submissive, and ladies, love always
He'll bless you in every way
just walk by faith
i sweat my calories away by faith
i feel better day by day
if you feel me say *hey*!
always walk by faith
and love the Lord in every way.

having faith will bless your walk.

black and beautiful

i'm black and beautiful
hot
like the sun
with smooth, brown skin
like coco butter.

i'm smart
blessed by the Best
favored
and attractive
with black, slanted eyes.
my identity is hidden
in my Heavenly Father.

i'm black and beautiful.

i'm loved and wonderfully made.
i'm blessed
kind
and beautiful on the outside and within.
true beauty is beyond what's in the mirror
it's deeper than my image, my art.

i'm black and beautiful
naked.
my identity is deeper
than my skin color.
i'm black and beautiful.

i'm confident in my skin.

inspired

one day i approached the parking lot when, sud-
denly, an older man walked up to my car with a
blue jacket, a fitted shirt showing his belly button,
stained pants and white shoes, white hair, a brown
cane, and a black backpack.

he had on reading glasses
and a beard white as snow.
but unlike Santa
in his right hand
he held up a half-emptied insulin bottle
and gave me an unexpected speech.
i sat with opened eyes and ears
and listened as i'd normally do
when my pastor preaches.
the words that he spoke touched my heart.
i was awake, not asleep
he was a human being
that could sit down and hear me teach.
i was shocked and meek.
i don't care if you think i'm a geek
wishing that somehow, he'd accept my heart
to feed him until he fell asleep.
he wanted more
so, i looked through my purse
and dug up some change.
listen
do anything that you can
to change the game, he's not to blame.
it's deeper than his shame.
i didn't laugh because it wasn't a joke or a game.
don't give or post on social media just to get the fame

just to claim that you aren't lame.
Lord knows he had no shame
he began to humble himself so he wouldn't walk away the
same.
the Lord showed up and came to his rescue with love, so
he'd give him the praise,
glory, and honor without delay.
do from the heart and pray for those who are homeless, sick,
and shut in.
then you'll leave your mark.
one that continues to make you stand out and shine
but after the veil is lifted.
so, don't be blind.
i'm inspired.

i'm always blown away by others.

God's plan

as human beings
created in an imperfect world
we live and plan
we strive to live perfect lives
as if we're birds in the tree
we think and maneuver
like CEOs.
we work and earn
to make a living
only to repeat the cycle
with or without God's plan
which is more powerful than a million fans.
this was my plan.
i walked without following the Manual
of life…i didn't advance
until God blessed me with another chance
He strengthened my faith.

i believed in the One, who created me
to do all that i can.

i love my calling.
i'm experiencing it, and it feels good
i'm satisfied, to God be the glory.

and i'm free.

He's mine, and i'm His child.
i'm taken by my Father
He is awesome.

i'm on track and living in God's plan.

i have faith.

desire God's plan.

in pain

i was in pain
it wasn't a game
month after month, it was all the same
they thought i would stay locked in this miserable chain.
i think i was going insane
but God's grace and mercy rescued me in my fast lane.
i wasn't to blame and wasn't ashamed to make a
claim.
they still didn't believe me
and nothing changed.
yes, i loved when he laid on top of me
shirtless
without underpants.
his love covered my pain
and comforted my spirit when i came.
He remained the same
of course, i know his name
i was in physical pain
no, i'm not ashamed
this is my song and testimony
thank you for listening while i sing
Christ said to me, "baby, it can't be the same.
change the game or i'll give you more pain. and
always remember my name."
i love to sing, *While the Blood is Running Warm in My Veins*
i'm no longer embarrassed.
i love to sing through my visible voice.
God gave me a choice
to divorce my remorse
with the right choice.
to speak through my visible voice.
He helped me make the right choice
He renewed my mindset.
transformed my heart.

i was in pain
but now i look back and thank God for transforming
my mind
i was in pain, but He came through and broke those
chains.
thank You, Lord.
i give you all the glory.
Amen.

my Father rescued me in His arms and made me feel better.

He's my heartbeat

my life is in the Lord
He gives me life
good health
and strength
He's my heartbeat.

i love the Lord with all my heart, mind
and soul—with all that i am
i really love the Lord
He's my heartbeat.

my life would be incomplete
without my Life Support
Jesus Christ
my Lord and Savior
He's the power in my walk
motivation in my blood
and inspiration in my calling
thank you, Lord

He's my heartbeat.

my life is in the Lord.

a woman's prayer

dear Lord,
thank you for grace and mercy
for life, health, and strength,
thank you for another day, another opportunity to live
in you and you alone
thank you for my loved ones and even my enemies
thank you for watching over my loved ones and protecting
them from any hurt, harm, or danger
thank you for making a way out of no way and watching
over
the sick and shut-in.
Lord, thank you for a roof over our heads, food to eat
and clothes on our backs.
thank you for keeping us and for your ever flowing provi-
sions,
and favor like no other
your power is making a way and strengthening me daily
as your child and as a woman, wife, and mother.

in Jesus' name, amen.

i'm a praying woman.

a wife's prayer

Lord,
thank you.
you knew me before i was born and loved me before i loved
myself.
thank you for creating me so wonderfully-made—in your
image.
no wonder i rejoice and praise your holy name—i'm in love
with me
and thankful for the woman and wife you designed me to
be, i am, and becoming.
i'm no longer afraid to shout in the middle of the road and
throw my hands
in the air and wave them like i just don't care.
i'm forever thankful and pray that you keep this zeal in my
heart—
an experience like no other.
Lord, i pray that you continue to bless every part of me that
makes me
who i was born to be—loving, caring, giving, outspoken,
bold, humble,
and fearless.
i pray i continue to be the best wife to my husband and sup-
port him unconditionally with love and compassion.
i pray i continue to submit to your will and surrender all of
me in Your hands.
we belong to you, so thank you and i appreciate you.
i pray i continue to worship and praise your name. Lord, i
give you all the glory
because you've been better to me than i've been to myself.
i seek you when it's light and dark—You're there and i'm
overjoyed.
help me to continue to be a submissive and strong

and to walk by faith. i'll honor You all the days of my life because You're worthy to be praised. Lord, thank You for opening my eyes when i needed you the most.
i pray they stay open, and You continue to strengthen me where i'm weak.
Lord, please watch over and protect my loved ones as well—we all need you more than ever. please forgive me for all my sins and guide me on Your path. Thank you for my husband, children, family, and friends. i trust in Your name and Your name alone. Your grace and mercy are powerful. i've got joy way down in my heart because i can smile, laugh and be me. You satisfy me. i'm a happy wife.

i'm blessed.

i adore her

i adore her like my heart
because she is my reflection—my shadow even when i'm
present—
and when we smile, laugh, and play together—that's me.
my daughter, my baby girl is my heart who i adore—
she's a gift like no other—
a blessing from God.
i adore her because she's precious like when she overcame
life
from my womb.
she's adorable, outgoing, kind, and a bundle of joy.
it's her i adore—my precious little girl whose smile lights
up the world
like the stars in the sky.
she's loved
and blessed.
she's sweet like the fruits i eat.
my lindsey girl, Kamaria, also loves to sing and dance, and
be the creative
little girl she was designed to be—before she was named.
she loves to eat and sleep and twirl on her tiny feet.
she's our world.
i love my precious little girl.
i adore her—my darling.
she's our bright little Lindsey girl.

we adore our precious little girl.

a mother's prayer

Lord,
thank you for Your grace and mercy and for blessing me
to be the best mother you created me to be.
i pray that i always live in You and walk in Your path.
Your love is more powerful than the world.
You get sweeter and sweeter as the days go by.
i pray i continue to be a loving and nurturing mother
Lord, thank you for disciplining me to be that mother You
created.
You motivate me and encourage me to be better, each day. i
love you.
Thank you, Jesus.

happy mother's day, each day.

i see

i see men and women, the young and old
walking down the streets on their feet and it's loud--
i feel your hurt and pain and understand that the struggle is
real.
i see your smiles and laughs and tears as you dance to the
beat
in the scorching heat with cigarettes and liquor near your
feet.
you're up near midnight.
i hear your loud voices
cries
and shouts.
you've been stopped
because they have no clue.
who created you
so, you're in the middle of the earth
winning
to get all they can out of you.
so they can glow
to get your brains twisted
and your hearts stirred.
i heard what happened
it was all over the news
because it's what they choose.
be strong, brave, loving
prayed up
and stay in school
because no one wants you to lose.
you're born winners and believe it or not
sinners
but through the blood of Jesus Christ
He's the only One who can make you right
just keep praying.

resist the devil
hang on
and never leave His sight.
i know you're bright.
only God judges with His sight.
so, be careful not to stare
show action
you were born with a heart full of fire in there
so, go sit down in that chair
sit up
and share what God has blessed you to overcome.
i know you're not dumb or a bum
there are some great men who've also sinned
you're not alone in this
make sure you hug your parents
and give them a kiss before you miss out on the time of your
life
it will become ripe with stripes
and blemishes but everything will improve
so, make sure to chill
and throw away those pills.
do you hear me?
life is serious but also, precious
don't take every heartbeat lightly
remember
there's a lot of tension in the world,
so, separate yourself from chaos
drama
and distractions.
pray for others and stay focused.
i empathize with you and know it causes stress.
you can't breathe nor concentrate
because your storms are getting the best of you.
i see, but God knows best.
He'll help you
and guide you safely in your storms.

so, be still and pray
keep your faith
and persevere with a smile.
one day freedom will have you
on your feet
rejoicing
and glorifying God for His power.
let go
and be strong
i see you.
you're not alone.

i see you. you're special.

memories

staring at you now
seems like yesterday.
when we laughed
outside of mom's tennis court.
i was there
with my mini speakers
microphone
tight, gray sweatpants
tennis shoes
blue live united t-shirt
sunglasses
with you near my side
like a special shadow
out of the blue.
we laughed and danced
and you helped me learn
how to improve my moves.
we grooved
we moved.
you said, "Kala, stick your butt out."
you need to do it and say it like this—
oh yes with the weather Lol.
you told me you loved the dance
and thought i should incorporate your version
as if you were amending the Constitution of the United
States.
i laughed and welcomed you to rock with me
dance with me
laugh with me
and speak into the mic
as if it was your show.
Allison had the most amazing glow

while we rocked with the flow.
she never said no.
we jammed together
despite her sometimes being low.
she was blessed and beautiful
with her cute afro
hazel eyes, brown hair, and the perfect little body.
she's more than a conqueror.
she's more than the smoke and smell that hovered over her
precious and special
body.
she's blessed and highly favored.
she's sweet
and determined.
she was smart.
she was more than a conqueror.
she had a heart filled with aspirations, love, compassion, and
forgiveness.
she worked hard
and sometimes enjoyed playing cards.
our memories will never fade.
she loved the shade
and sitting by the pool
meditating and relaxing.
it was her rule
and sleeping in the cool
she wasn't no fool
she stayed in school
and was determined
our memories will never fade.

Allison's spirit is unforgettable.

true beauty

true beauty is beyond your appearance
it's deeper than the layers of your skin
and the tattoos on your arm.
true beauty overpowers it.
it dominates your eyelashes and mountain-cut eyebrows
and the beauty marks on your chest.
it's more precious than your lips, eyes, and beautiful hair.
and it's not the clothes that you wear
the lingerie
skinny jeans
ripped shirts
leather shoes
and everything that covers your body.
true beauty is beyond your smile
and eye-catching dimples.
true beauty shines
like the sun and stars in the sky.
it reflects your heart
true beauty is deep.

true beauty is more powerful than your skin.

the confident woman

when she awakes
she prays with gratitude
because she knows
who controls her feet.
that's why she loves
her walk down the street.
she teaches
and speaks.
she's meek
and loves to dance on her feet
to the sounds of her heartbeat of confidence
with peace
freedom
a smile and a turn.
everyone hears the sound
of her powerful steps.
they know who it is.
her presence is felt
and soft like her.
they know she's not weak
she's confident
blessed from the inside out
from her head to her heels
by the Best.

be confident.

the taste of freedom

as i laid down in silence
i saw the moon shining as white as snow
it was beautiful like a little shiny bow
it had the perfect glow
but that wasn't all.
i was also amazed at how the stars surrounded it
like a crowd of butterflies.
Lord knows i was ready to for my deliverance.
i knew after this hour i was going to overcome life.
i would continue to grow.
it didn't matter how slow
i knew i would still glow.
then, suddenly, i was out.
i slumbered without a snore.
my heart was heavy
i felt it inside
like weights falling on my head.
i was covered in the most colorful sheets.
i loved gazing at my daughter's feet
her and my husband were asleep.
but what a crazy and chaotic week.
my heart was noisy
like the sound of hearing a beginner choir of clarinet play-
ers.
day one was forte
and day two was fortissimo
my heart was noisy.
i was restless
until i was finally awakened before dawn.
something extraordinary happened, and i feel good
i feel like a brand new me
it's unexplainable but explainable.

i experienced a *but God* moment
and i'm certain it'll last forever
to God be the glory
i can breathe now.
i'm free.

i'm free and this i know.

asleep

i'm asleep—but who knows?
well, i don't, but i'm sure God does.
it's dark and i can't see—not even in the mirror
i only see me and it's strange
because my vision is unusual—it's blurry
and its been this way for years.

the only things i see are images of obstacles
and hardships of life—my own reality.

everything sucks—being broke and depressed is no good
scene.

i was undercover
but now the curtains have been removed
my mood was disguised
only to let my makeup cover
my greatest fears
disappointments
shame
depression
and embarrassments
but my attitude
heart
and spirit embraced life
with gratitude and appreciation.
i grew stronger than
five pounds of weights
and flourished
despite being lower than the foundation of the oceans.
i was in a world of bondage

like a caged bird
surrounded by
disobedience
sin
and lacked discipline.
my atmosphere
was stinking and
surrounded by fog
that kept me distracted
down
and distanced
from others
afraid to express my own feelings
afraid to smile
laugh
and express my true colors
of joy and excitement.
but i knew one day God would open my eyes
from such a world
that many are still trapped in today
the same world
where i couldn't see anything
except for the color black.

spiritual darkness
invaded my innocent and precious body.
it settled on my flesh and bones
ran through my veins.
i was conscious
but unconscious, and it took over my life.
i felt like a walking bomb
that would explode on any given day
but God delivered me.

freedom called my name
from out of this lifeless, quiet, yet loud and lonely tunnel
awakening from bondage.
i served my flesh with a veil
dark as the night skies that led me on a
journey of confusion, frustration, guilt, and depression.
sheets covered my body like a mummy.
i was blind
lost and nowhere to be found
except laying down in a tunnel filled with darkness.
i was restless.
there was something about my aching heart
that was worth rejoicing about and sharing with you.
i was awakened
by the noise of my desperate and dying being
with joy, excitement, gratitude, humility, and fire
to pick up a pen and start writing my story
my testimony of freedom and the grace, mercy, and good-
ness of God
days after i experienced life on the ground
without the ability to move and catch my breath
as if i were in the ring with Mohammad Ali.
i fought knowing the battle was the Lord's, and He
won.
He came through and blessed my soul
in the midst of a job loss.
His unconditional love and power shifted me
in an unimaginable place in my life
and i'm forever grateful.
however, i was at rock bottom, on the ground, lost again
until i chose to do what i needed to do
and that was to give up my life, surrender
and submit to my Lord and Savior
who renewed my mindset—my heart

then blessed me to experience freedom from the bondage of
this world.
to this day, the Lord has been ever on my lips.
i thank God that i was awakened.

i can see, hallelujah.

love

the love hour

i love this:
as he walks through the door
the wind behind him attracts my senses
and smells stronger than the smell of
garlic and herbs simmering in the apart-
ment.
his smell is sweeter than the freshest blueberries
but sometimes unpleasant
like the smell of an athlete
after a four-hour super bowl game.
but i'm okay with it.
i love his smell.
it turns me on, and so does he.
i'm use to it, and he's use to
the sweat that drips from my chest after a long workout in
the gym.
he wins me over every time.
his smell is never bitter like lime.
it's wild
recognizable
hot
and attractive to my brains
even when it rains.
i have no shame.
my heart is the same—
love runs through my veins.
i know it's time for the love hour
a special moment like no other.
it's time to make love.
he's ready and so am i.
my heart is smiling with butterflies.
i love his body scent
he turns me on like the first day we met.

i know who's in my presence
i can't wait for the love hour.
so, i rise from first base
wearing a t-shirt and gym shorts.
i'm in the mood
and sure, he's ready to get it on
in the voice of Marvin Gaye.
especially during the love hour.
so, i pace to the bathroom with a smile
except hidden underneath my pretty, brown skin, long eye-
lashes, and slanted eyes
though it's exposed seconds before the love hour.
i can't wait for the love hour.
not to watch the New Year's ball drop near the beach
not dinner at the resort and suits
not Friday's date night heat.
i can't wait for the love hour.
a special hour when grownups make love.
sisters, i get goosebumps when he doesn't wear a glove.
i love when he's inside of me—i'm in heaven.
and oh, how i love the sweat that falls from his face.
it hits my risk
then the sound of love
like an audience
clapping their hands
enters my ears.
it's the love hour.
there's nothing like it.
my wrist and fingers grab the couch.
he kisses my neck.
i shout his name with no one else on my mind.
i'm focused on him.
he's the most handsome man in my space.
it's the love hour.

then he holds me by the waist and takes over my backseat.
i love when he smacks my ass like bouncing a ball.
it's the love hour.
we explode like fireworks
kiss
and smile at each other.
i submit to my king
as i submit to Christ
we're free
and thankful for the love hour.

we love this hour; it's one of our favorites.

a song without words

--------be silent---------

inhale and exhale. embrace it. enjoy it.

dear prisoner,

although i've never seen your face
i can only imagine
the pain and emotional headache
you're experiencing with your black, blue, brown, and gray
eyes
that first opened
when you were born
from your mother's womb.
they're closed now.
but nevertheless
it's not the end of the world.
you were created
and born on purpose
with purpose
and blessed for a greater purpose.
so long for it
now
today
and forever.
long to rise above your afflictions
and dream to mount up
with wings despite the storms of life
and before you overcome life passing through this dark tun-
nel.
God knows you're struggling in darkness
so, have hope and faith.
He is the Light
before
during
and at the end of the tunnel.
keep dreaming
while praying that your dreams
become a reality.

i pray they do
starting today
and every second after.

i can only imagine the outside
but i empathize with you
because i can only paint a picture
of your insides
the body that God created before life even began
so precious
sensitive
beautiful
and wonderfully made
yet powerful enough to make a difference.
have faith.
you will experience freedom.
not just out of these painful gates
and dark walls of suffering
but through the blood of Jesus Christ.
surrender and submit no more to that route.
there's a safer, more powerful, and better
way
and that's by following the Way, Truth, and
Life.
so, don't give up.
stay prayed up.
keep the faith.
keep smiling.
and praise the Lord.

dear prisoner,
there's hope
light
freedom
life
blessings

and there's a taste better and more powerful than your daily
meal
seek to experience it
seek to know it
seek to surrender and submit to it
seek to follow it
and seek to share and encourage someone else about it.
to experience this taste is far more pleasing than Campbell's
delicious soup
what's your favorite?
let it be the Word
Jesus Christ, our Lord and Savior
God, our Creator
God, our Healer
God, our Miracle Maker
God, our Chain Breaker.

dear prisoner,
stay strong and never give up.
i have never seen your face, but i can imagine your eyes.
pray that He opens them.
you can do it.
but God will make it happen.
dear prisoner,
have faith over fear.

May God bless you with freedom.

you're not alone

i see you walking near the supermarket
on the sidewalk
looking for something to eat.
i know you feel alone.

i see it in your face
and in your body gestures.
you're broke and feel broken
betrayed and empty
lost and lonely
like your neighbor
except you're homeless
and feel helpless.
it hurts, and i know it does.
but you're not alone.

i also see you on corner streets

past midnight
while everyone is asleep
and drinking in their backyards
dancing to beats
making loud noises in their jeeps
you feel hopeless.
i know it's difficult.
but you're not alone.

you stand near the playground
solo
with filthy clothes and marks on your face
through winter, spring, summer, and fall.
you pray without giving up
because you're strong.
you inspire others
when your hands touch
and cry out to our Heavenly Father.

you have hope because better days are coming.
i know it's not easy.
you're not alone.

i also saw that sheet
and broken seat
with your precious
little brown feet.
you were hungry

so, you looked in the dumpster
and found something to eat
it was unpleasant
but you did what you had to do
before you went to sleep

you slept and slumbered
so, i prayed to God
that He'd protect you.

i know many walked around you
for whatever reasons.
they overlooked your beautiful, precious heart.

never give up.
you're not alone
walking through the bushes
in the scorching heat
eating on your knees
and laying in parking lots.
you're not alone under the bridge.
surrender your all to Him
and He'll guide you on the right path.

everything will be okay. you're not alone.

Allison

as i stood and stared at her
precious, hazel eyes
i smiled
with faith
and confidence
certainty that she'd overcome such a battle
a life event that stands before her precious
body
Lord willing
as she laid wrapped in sheets
white as snow.
Allison is blessed
one of a kind
and impossible to miss
her heart
it's beautiful
and sings louder than her visible voice.
she's a woman
her name is Allison
she's sweet like honey
compassionate
clothed with grace and mercy
and carries a loving spirit
her story inspires many
like a tunnel that's lit
by the Light
she's forever loved
her name is Allison.

she's one of a kind.

he's my teddy bear

he's my teddy bear.
when i'm cold he's there.
he keeps me warm in the cool air.
man, i love his cute dimples and wavy hair.
and oh, i love when he stares
when my legs are crossed
while sitting in the chair.
he also loves my hair.
and turns me on
when we're texting and talking on the phone.
when he sits
i always see his glare.
i get goosebumps.
he's no longer the man that gets crump.
i said Amen hallelujah
he's my teddy bear.
when we're together, we smile
laugh
embrace each other and the love we share.
when i need him, he's there
he has my back, and i have his.
i love his affection.
when we touch
his hugs and kisses turn me on
like during the love hour.
we love to express ourselves
when we're under the sheets
we love to make love.
i love my teddy bear.
sometimes i just stare
thanking God for His grace and mercy.
we're blessed.

i'm one lucky, happy woman.
thank you, Lord.
You satisfied my soul
i'm pleased with your grace.
i'm married to the sweetest teddy bear.
i love you.

we're love birds.

in labor

it's after midnight and i'm tossing in bed like a milkshake
i'm turning—left to right like something is wrong

my head feels like it's going to fall off...or stay on
with all this tension—what in the hell is going on
hello in there—can anybody here me—why am i moving
like this
what is happening to me—am i going nuts before i give up
on life
or will someone talk to me?

dear heart,
are you okay or not? you're acting strange. you're anxious.
what's going on?

the only sound i hear is my noisy, cranky heart
like the sound of a loud engine.
it's something serious
but i don't know what it is.
i'm clueless and restless
like a crying baby who's unable to rest
in the midst of a quiet environment—in silence.

i was just fired or should i say
my job was taken away out of nowhere (but somewhere in
this world)
like a bunch of aliens who just took over the whole planet—
strange right?
well, this is a problem. houston, do you hear me?
now i'm wide awake and i don't
know what to do
so, now what?

i'm hurting, deep down and it doesn't feel good.
it feels like something sharp is poking my brain like a
thorn—
something painful, but possibly powerful.

i don't have a stomach ache—it's bigger than that
like the heart of thirty million planets.
i wanna rest, but you're loud in there.
you're noisy and anxious about something
and i wanna know—i'm curious
like Curious George.

well, in silence my fingers are moving on the keypad—
swiftly
and i'm focused on nothing except releasing words that
tell my story—my journey of this unbelievable day—words
from the heart.

ouch—this hurts but i must keep going before dawn.
writing almost a thousand pages was emotionally challeng-
ing
but satisfying.
i didn't need a tylenol
i needed to release my heart
like garbage in my life.
every time i empty it
it's fulfilling.
God transformed my mindset
and blessed my life.
i'm in a different place now
an extraordinary environment
i love my space.
i get to let go

i'm free, and it feels good.
i love expressing myself and being
creative—me—genuine and sassy.
my delivery was worth the pain but also joy.
it was special
it was an unforgettable experience.

i was in labor with my calling.

inspired in silence

i'm inspired in silence
to do the things that encourage and motivate me to keep
going
without ever giving up
and even if i do
i always see the light at the end of the tunnel
with every color
except black
because the Light always replaces it
with hope.
i'm inspired in silence to read, write, smile, dance, exercise,
pray, persevere,
and spread love.
i'm inspired in silence to never quit
despite days i want to give up
and rest.
dark days and days when nothing
makes sense.
i'm inspired in silence to stand strong
courageous
humble and confident
knowing that with Christ
all things are possible.
i'm inspired to write what's stuck
buried
and clogged in my heart
in the depths of my flesh
and bones to expose
express
and embrace my experiences
to encourage and help others.
i'm inspired in silence
to fear the Lord and walk by faith

with gratitude and appreciation.
i'm inspired to seek God and His righteousness.
i'm inspired to live one day at a time
to pray without ceasing
and to never give up.
i'm inspired in silence to embrace the process.

i love listening to my heartbeat.

my partner

he's tall like the Statue of Liberty
and brown like my thighs
which also reflect the skin color around
my beautiful, slanted eyes.
my partner is built
and handsome.
i love to see him get undressed
and stand in the shower.
he's all mine and i'm all his.
he says i'm fine.
he turns me on and loves when i call his name
during the love hour.
he's my partner
my helpmeet.
his sweat makes me wet
and elevates my heart rate
when we're together like peanut butter and jelly
on the bed
on the floor
in the bathroom
on the kitchen counter
or on the couch.
he's sweet
and confident in the ring.
he no longer walks with bling.
i love him so much.
i'm comforted by his touch
and smile when i see his dimples.
i'm in love with my king because he keeps it simple.
he's sweet.
my partner is loved.
i know i'm his shadow.

i always glow.
he's sweet
like the fruits we eat
apples, oranges, bananas, and vegetables like sweet tomatoes and beats.
fruits are my favorite
but he loves crackers before he goes to sleep
the kind everyone likes to eat
but he doesn't like sweets
my goodies are his treats.
when he says this, i can feel the heat.
we love to make love, laugh, and then eat
and no, he's not cheap.
he's a real man
disciplined
and god-fearing.
he's precious, kind, and loving.
he doesn't drive a jaguar or some luxurious car.
he's content with a vehicle.
he loves to chill and listen to his favorite beats.
thank you, Lord.
i love my partner.
i blush and get butterflies even while he's sleep
i giggle and we kiss.
he's my partner.
he's handsome and sweet.

my partner is sweet like dark chocolate.

you're loved

depression, loneliness, betrayal, and guilt are overpowering
your life
and you don't feel loved
like a cage bird being abandoned.
don't worry.
you are loved
beyond your chaotic resident
of the sidewalk and tricky nights
of trying to overcome the path
of abuse
sexual harassment
drug and alcohol addiction
prostitution
molestation
and domestic violence
listen up
you are loved and i'm certain
because your smile
continues to radiate through your spirit
you don't look like how you feel.
your love continues
to brighten up others' day
your compassion
continues to bless your heart
and your perseverance
continues to motivate
and inspire your neighbors
and strangers.
as we look at a distance
we're moved to continue living
with a heart of gratitude
we're encouraged to continue giving and

being a blessing to others
and we're filled with joy and happiness to
continue living a selfless life
you're loved.

God loves you.

i'm a woman of color without color

i'm a woman of color without color
black with brown skin
with a temple born into sin
but blessed to win
i'm black and beautiful.

i'm a god-fearing woman of color without color
who was created, wonderfully made, and blessed by
God with purpose, passion, and power.
my confidence is deeper than the color of my skin
i'm inspired.

i'm a beautiful woman of color without color
born to fight with human rights
and blessed to overcome life.
i no longer wear a disguise
i'm finally living with open eyes
with strength to rise.
i'm black and beautiful.

i'm a woman of color without color
who was born from a mother
who's also a woman of color
without color.

i'm a beautiful woman.

searched for love

black with brown skin
ordinary like your neighbor
i was that teenager
who wore regular clothes and searched for love in the world
like watching children run
and play hide and seek
with the speed of a track star runner.
i thought love was the main sense
so, i embraced what i smelt
and heard
tasted
saw
and felt
with anxiety and goosebumps that ran
on my brown-skinned arms.
i never had to clock in because i searched
for love beyond dark hours
which made midnight and early mornings were
my favorites because i was exposed to the best love making
ever
like tasting the richest banana pudding in the world.
i clocked in
without ever taking a vacation
because i fell in love in such a tunnel of captivity.
i searched for love and associated love with a magnetic
body
that kept me hooked and high
orgasm after orgasm
as if it was a children's game, experiencing imitation and
fun
yet i played without toys and made a lot of noise.
my ears were attracted to the sound of love
and my body was attracted to his soft and pale skin
and the hairs on his body intertwined with mine
but never turned loose

as if growing was part of the plan.
i searched for love beyond
many nights of making love as
a chef prepares and carefully bakes.
it was hot and heavy
but disappointment proceeded after mealtime.
the show was over but started again as if i was on a difficult
contract without lasting
benefits.
everything went fast like watching a motorcyclist speed
around block thirteen
a million times without change
progress
improvement
and purpose.
i searched for love until i finally understood the game.
i stopped opening the oven and letting my addiction simmer
in
where i desired.
i wanted the lights on.
i was tired of sitting behind the stove watching sin excite my
precious and blessed body.
i desired life in order and discipline
to continue teaching me how to love, breathe, and flourish
with true love.
at that moment, the veil was removed from the caramel cake
and flesh
no longer searching for love on the east in the best suites.
love rescued me and guided my mind, body, and soul as i
exited the dark tunnel
of captivity
love there was easy, hidden, and convenient, beyond dark
chocolate on
vanilla ice cream.
i heard His voice and followed the true way of love

i searched for Love and found
my Heavenly Father.

i found true Love.

precious

when i looked at her face
it was brown and shiny
as if she had been sitting
out in the sun watching the bumble bees fly around
by the beautiful waterside pool area
not a drop of sweat came running down her face
except the expression she made at a screen
and she almost cried
"don't cry, Allison," but my mother said, "no, it's okay.
let her express herself."
i was shocked but also wide-eyed staring at the reality of
sitting on the other side while overlooking a loved one on a
bed covered in white sheets and a towel that gave her extra
support on the left side of her face.
i expressed empathy
and gazed into her eyes
with hopes that she'd overcome this battle
so she'd see the sun again
like the day she was delivered from my mother's womb
when she first overcame life from God's hands.
i heard sounds of our childhood
where we laughed and sometimes cried.
she's human
imperfect
with flaws.
she's special
precious
blessed
and one of a kind.
she's greater than her past
she's strong
and a hard, fighting soldier
she's human.

she rocks the world.

the sound of life

the sound of life has my attention like my husband when
he's on top
or the opposite
or even when he's in the shower.
my ears are open like my eyes.
i'm curious and interested
as i lay under my cozy
colorful
and thick sheets
amid the peace and quiet.
my mind is relaxed
motivated
and constantly inspired
by the sound of life—
from hearing the cool breeze
outside my apartment window
wind as it hits the tree
that stands in front of the complex
cars driving and honking
neighbors talking
and laughing outside
couples having sex
and hearing
the alarms ring as if life was timeless.

listen because there's beauty in what you're hearing.

my heart is free

it's big, powerful, and imperfectly shaped—
my heart is more valuable and purposeful
than the clothes over my pretty, brown skin—
my arms, chest, and thighs can never compare to my phe-
nomenal heart
and my skinny jeans and sleeveless shirts doesn't define
who i am because my heart will forever be stronger
than what you see—my heart is more impactful than opin-
ions.
my heart is free.
it's no longer imprisoned in darkness.
i can finally see.
my heart is free.

i'm stronger than ever.

on the edge

hello, can anybody hear me out there?
i'm young, single, and broke and i'm living on the edge—
i keep crashing my head and i'm tired—
fed up with living paycheck to paycheck—
i'm on the edge of not having enough because i'm financial-
ly blind—
i don't know what to do with this green God is giving me
so it's everywhere—i think it's a game because i'm always
losing
more than i earn—i'm living on the edge and i've barely
started college—
i have more debt than i've earned in a lifetime—help—i'm
on the edge
and i'm about to lose it—my car and everything else—
i'm on the edge of losing my life insurance—i'm on the
edge and i need some
discipline, some spiritual direction—i give but then take
away—
i'm hiding what belongs to God—could this be it or what?
what in the hell is going on here? it seems like i'm walking
in circles—
year after year—i've graduated from college, but i'm still
broke—
i'm living on the edge; its been decades and i can't seem to
be free—
delivered from this edge—financial hell.
i'm tired of living on the edge and it's tough—
it's a struggle and one of the scariest experiences ever.
i feel like i'm at the top of a mountain with burdens on my
shoulders—
stuff like trials and tribulations, money problems and all
and i can't move because i'm in a mess that i keep facing

every time i try to do right—on this journey of life—
i'm short—i have less than what i started with--
i'm on the edge of giving up... it's too much, but...
i won't because i have hope and faith.

it's a new day and i'm one step further than i was yester-
day—
i'm in a better position on this edge than i was years ago—
the edge will always exist because i've chosen not to live on
the edge—
i've chosen to have faith and trust in the Lord than to live on
the edge.

He delivered me from the edge.

somebody

i'm single and praying i meet a respectful, young man—
unlike the ones i've met in the past…somebody different—
somebody who'll love me for me, for who God created me to be--
god-fearing, fearfully, and wonderfully made
and nothing less as if i'm a piece of trash or lifeless hu-man—an instrument
for sex, fun, and play and then garbage.

i'm praying for somebody, a man, who'll love me
like Christ, and not for anything under my clothes—
i know about these guys—it's unbelievable, but real.

i don't want anybody.
i need a man…that special somebody who i can grow old with
and who'll treat me like a young lady—not somebody who craves my body
more than they desire a relationship with Christ.

i'm praying for somebody who valuables my heart and de-sires to become one.

hello world…i'm waiting patiently for my boaz—
i know he's on his way so i'm praying for that day
when God unites him with me—somebody special.

the clock is ticking…

it's over a decade and here i am—
i'm still here and still standing.
i'm looking in the mirror and praying for somebody—that

spouse—not just anybody—but somebody God-sent.

i know He's listening and will answer my prayers.
my faith will prove it. yay!

it finally happened…. He made it happen—God blessed me
with somebody and i'm thankful—to God be the glory.
He blessed me with the god-fearing man
i prayed for without ever knowing he'd be the one
until now.

God blessed me with a real man.

Kala Jordan-Lindsey

when it's quiet...

i hear dogs barking and loud music at the top of the roof
as if a concert was happening—in a complex of a hundred
units—
in the middle of the night.
when it's silent
i hear my heartbeat over a million others
whose heart seems noisy, anxious, and stressed
like a mother's who's restless as she worries about
life—tomorrow and what the future holds for her and her
family.
when it's quiet
i'm inspired by the noise of life, people, and their frustra-
tions
over the struggles of this race.

it's mind blowing when it's quiet.

i hear babies crying, doors being shut
and anger from humanity when blood stains and wombs
are shown through innocent men and women,
boys and girls of color, who lay on the ground
without breath
without life to enjoy and embrace life again.

when it's quiet i hear body parts on the street.
i hear somebody walking and running.
i hear men laughing and shouting on fridays
and checkers thrown on tables.
when it's quiet
i hear loud women
foul language
and the sound of men and women
and beds

vibrating above my ceiling and against my walls.

when it's silent
my heart is relaxed
attentive
focused
and calm.

in silence
i'm at peace.
in silence
comfort runs to my rescue
with love

hope
and faith.
i'm in love in silence.
i smile and love to laugh in silence.
i hear my Father when it's quiet.

i accomplish things when it's quiet.

in my mother's womb

before birth, i was curled in my mother's womb
like a seashell on the sand
near the atlantic ocean
except i was closer.
i was hidden in the walls of my mother's placenta
in darkness, i lay as an unborn gift
created by an awesome God
who knew me before i was born.
i moved in proximity to my mother's exit door
and endured wiggles and turns.

it was days, weeks, and months where i was entrapped
in darkness, in a human body where it was secluded--what a
journey,
an experience i can only imagine
with a glimpse of light and hope at the end of the tunnel
surrounded by unusual and unexpected blessings
that were intentional.
i only laid in my mother's womb to execute what was pre-
pared, set, and settled in
the Book of Life to happen at such a perfect time.
i posed while laying down on my stomach
in my mother's womb
as if i were taking a selfie
lights, cameras, action, baby
and sometimes, i laid on my back
in fetal position
in the depths of my mother's placenta

only because i wasn't stabled.
i enjoyed rocking the world.
the bigger and stronger i grew
i moved like a squirming worm
at a pace as fast as a tiger
but then i turned back in the opposite direction on purpose
with purpose
and for a greater purpose.
i was floating on top of the world
before i was delivered into this world
it was all about me, myself, and i
before i overcame life from my mother's womb.
i had a ball
gulping down all the nutritional picture-less foods
that satisfied my tiny little belly.
it was the size of my father's fist
and i never resisted my food parties.
i knew it was intentional
food was essential
and i knew i had to grow.
i wasn't slow and never did i know
except my anticipation to exit my mother's womb.
i never signed up to remain in complete darkness or regis-
tered in the army of
unborn babies to hide and never be seen
to never walk in my purpose
and execute in my life calling
but in my mother's womb.
God created me with a plan, purpose
and power to cross over to the other side
to succeed in life
to taste food but to also
experience His goodness, grace, and mercy
favor found and only given by Him

to taste His strength and power
to taste obstacles impossible for man to handle except with
Him.
i waited quietly to experience life
without a word spoken
except with my body gestures and growth.
i kicked and flipped
and tried to escape a claustrophobic body
but it wasn't time.

i wasn't ready
so, i continued to float around the darkness
of my mother's womb
with closed eyes and a naked, innocent, precious, special,
strong, and blessed body
as i fought with defeat every time
against every obstacle i faced.
my struggles motivated me
and adversity drove me to persevere
in my anxious little body
with determination to overcome life
from my mother's womb in silence, a deserted place.
i sat patiently, waiting to be rescued and delivered from my
mother's womb
in silence.

i overcame life through my mother's womb.

rock bottom

laying down in a puddle of tears
felt like i wasted so many years
because i chose to create these hills—a lot of bills.
but i thank God i never popped any pills.
so many chose this route and got killed.
i know that overtime
we wouldn't have to continue in the grind
because the Lord knows when it's our time.
i don't wanna look behind every day—i'm trying
i'm not lying
like an eagle.
i'll continue flying, soaring beyond my days of crying.
i'll continue to heal
and Lord willing
pay off this student loan bill.
i'm just keeping it real.
hitting rock bottom made me ill.
but leaning on the Lord strengthened me with an
amazing refill.
He renewed my mindset, which has given me
unstoppable zeal.
i thank God that we can finally pay bills.
His love always fulfills our heart's desires and
keeps you walking with the same zeal.
i pray, relax, and just chill.
my family and i never miss a meal.
hitting rock bottom
gave me a chance to live and be still
then God blessed me in His will and revealed my pur-
pose and life calling
i'm forever fulfilled because now i'm living
in His will.

it blessed me.

thank You, Lord

i'm sitting at my desk with a smile as big as the universe—
because i'm overjoyed and thankful—Thank You, Lord
with a list as long as the longest bridge in the world
and as wide as the entire galaxy.

i could never thank You enough
even if i bought a million cards on every
holiday of the year
and published a billion books that were hidden with my
signature
i could never thank You as much as i desire.
Lord, i am nothing without You.
thank You for grace and mercy.
Lord, You are my song.

joy is housed in my heart.

survivor

i'm a survivor
because i was awakened this morning
to God be the glory
i'm a survivor
because my heart is still beating
i'm thankful
i'm a survivor
because i made it out of bed
my God is awesome
i'm living because of His grace and mercy
i'm overjoyed
because the blood is running warm
through my veins
and my heart
is beating to the pace of a clock
it's healthy
i'm a survivor
because every bone created in me
and a part of me is still connected
i'm blessed
i'm a survivor
because i'm walking
what a mighty God
i'm a survivor
because i wasn't killed last night
praise the Lord
i'm a survivor
because i didn't commit suicide yesterday
i'm living in my right mind
i'm a survivor
because i didn't jump off the highest mountain in the world
i'm a survivor

because i made it home safe today
i'm a survivor
because i made it home safe after my honeymoon
glory to God
i'm a survivor
because i didn't have a heart attack when i was supposed to
i'm a survivor
because i wasn't diagnosed with cancer
we're survivors
because my family and i still have a roof over our heads
and food to eat
i'm a survivor
because i have money in the bank
praise God
i'm a survivor
because i overcame depression
to God be the glory
i'm a survivor
because i never smoked weed nor drank alcohol
i'm a survivor
because i lost my job but not my gifts
i'm a survivor
because God kept me safe during my entire pregnancy
glory to God
i'm a survivor because i haven't quit
i'm a survivor because i'm still standing
to God be the glory for His grace
and mercy.

i'm a survivor and so are you.

noises

i hear noises
from sunrise to sunset
pleasant and unpleasant
loud and soft.
i hear alarm clocks
school buses
honking cars
the train
loud voices of women, men
and children laughing and playing
on their electronic devices
and crying babies
thirsting for milk
pacifiers
toys
or for a mother's touch.
crossing guards
making the loudest sounds
on the streets
train arrivals and departures
airplane engines
motorcycles
city busses
dumpster trucks
police and ambulance sirens
all vibrating my ears.
boom blasting in your neighborhood
a college student or child practicing on
their trumpet
violin
or piano.
your wife singing in the shower

and the sound of couples making love
the sounds of life
engage
motivate
inspire
encourage
and uplift
like that of hearing your favorite artist
live in concert.
the sounds of life
help keep man alive
breathing
building
bonding
and blessing each other
the sounds of life
and voices of human beings
what a world we live in
today
the sounds of life.

listen to life.

the woman in front of the mirror

the woman in front of the mirror
is far more beautiful, blessed, bold, and built with a special,
contagious, and loving spirit beyond the woman in the mir-
ror who really gives grace
and invites others into her place
who's protective of her space
humble without ever
having to chase everything
below outer space
and looks beyond just the race
but sometimes she covers her face
so that no man could ever see the trace
of her rough life
and dreams of taking a knife
but she never gave up
God blessed her
to finally become a wife
though she still sometimes covers her face
and the true colors of her race
by using a lot of base
to cover up what her heart really wants to say
but now she prays
with more confidence and gratitude
with a positive attitude and appreciation
beyond what others have to say
she does it anyway
knowing that God will always make a way
she's fearless
courageous
and bold beyond gold
that continues to flourish
and nourish the hearts
of the young and old

she's clothed
without the mold and gold that once filled
her body and soul, she's the woman in
front the of the mirror.

you're beautiful, so exist.

grace

i'm somebody, a human being, but i don't know who i am
because i haven't been born—i'm still swimming around
in my mother's womb and on some days like mornings and
nights, my body is curved
like a shell—i'm this way because i'm not ready to be re-
leased—
something is holding me down until i get the green light
to go, to kick and turn, and do back flips in my mother's
stomach
i'm near that stage though—how exciting, right?

i'm ready to see this small but big world
and i can't wait, so i'm going to do everything possible to
get my
mom's attention since i can't yell—
i'm somebody, a human, being, but i don't know who i am
until i get out of here and finally figure out my identity—
at some point in my lifetime—i'm thinking maybe years
from now
after i've struggled with life enough, hit rock bottom, and
almost
gave up on my life, just like that…we shall see.

but hey, mama, it's time and i'm ready to see the world
like a tourist traveling to the top of the mountain.
finally, it's the hour and by the grace of God, i was delivered
i overcame life in such a dark, secluded place—my mother's
womb
after struggling with life for nearly nine months
and i can't leave out that the umbilical cord got wrapped
around
my neck and i almost went to heaven—i almost died

but grace saved me—to God be the glory.

but this wasn't the end—grace protected me and blessed me
throughout my life journey—every day and all day
like the love i continue to receive—it never fails, it never
runs out like His grace but also God's mercy.

i struggled with life since birth like a drunk person
that never stopped drinking until something life-threating
happened…
grace covered me and i realized it
when i continued to face obstacles and everything else
that humans experience.

His grace and mercy saved me.

i embrace my tattoo.

yesterday

today seems like yesterday
when i was half the size i am now.
i was petite and wore pigtails
and twist that engaged the whole world
but it was only yesterday that i was that little girl in those
shoes
that ran like a race car and smiled when i saw you.
i was that little, black girl with slanted eyes, who stuttered
when i released my tongue in front of everyone i knew.

it took me almost a year to say one word—
i struggled with this speech impediment like i was in the
ring
with my heart and tongue.

my voice stayed on mute in my heart—
it lived there and there alone without ever traveling
until it was time for me to talk, to make sound
so, i often traveled, which took a while
but i rarely used my mouth unless i had to.
i enjoyed hiding in my own body—in my heart
because i wasn't enthused about expressing myself
in the position where i stumbled over my own words
but i finally won—i overcame this long, tiresome fight
by the grace and mercy of God.

this hour also seems like yesterday
when i was a naive adolescent who was lost and blind
in a dark world where left and right seemed correct—the
right ways to go--
when everything looked and tasted good
in the sight of my heart.

i was inexperienced so i desired the experience
because my flesh controlled my heart and feelings.
however, as i became taller—as i matured
i became conscious of left and right and started making
better choices in my life
i started to learn about God, our Creator
so, i became more confidence and my self-esteem grew
stronger.

today no longer seems like yesterday
because now i have a better understanding of yesterday

i understand everything happened on purpose
with purpose, and for a greater purpose.
yesterday was yesterday, so now i live for today
with open eyes—wisdom from the Lord
which helps me embrace my yesterday and prepares me for
today.

yesterday helps me today.

the cry

from sunrise to sunset
i hear the cry—loud sounds of pain and agony from human-
ity
(from men and women, boys, and girls)
while birds chirp near my window as the earth spins
around and around like the repetitive circle i walked in—
in the wilderness—nonstop until i became conscious of my
life.

i hear many voices and it's coming from everywhere—from
the north, east, south, and west—all over the land and it's
getting louder…
on the streets where many sleep and pray,
under secluded bridges where many sell drugs and drink
alcohol,
in the projects where many are poor and have less than
you'd ever imagine,
on the premises of closed businesses and in front of busi-
nesses,
at government centers where the doors are locked with mil-
lions beyond their budgets and projected earnings,
outside of food markets and at stop lights and stop signs
near the white house
and near many who have more than they'd ever live to en-
joy God's grace.

the cry is never disguised but exposed without a veil…on
purpose.

do you hear the roar? listen and pray…

the cry is from man—
from the frustration of living in poverty
being jobless then becoming homeless.
many are in a crisis because they're living on a fixed income
without medical care and retirement savings—

they're struggling to put food on the table and keep their heads above water.

the cry is louder than yesterday when the only news we see is our black men and black boys being shot—it's ridiculous—it's senseless—
it's hateful…

we're dealing with spiritual warfare and it's real…

many are screaming for help where help is not given
the cry is seen in countries where many are
suffering from sex trafficking, sexual harassment
immigration, a lack of education and health care opportunities

and the omission of prayer in schools.

the cry is real.

the nation is hurting.

addicted

he wore light, soft colors
and some were dark—
his shirts were attractive to my blind eyes.
i loved his favorite songs and adored when he
drove down my street—

looking at his handsome face gave me goosebumps
every time and butterflies that made me wet like the sweat
that drips from my face after a long run on the track field.

when i saw him, i smiled—
his appearance attracted my black, slanted eyes
i was in love with him—
this stranger, not because of his money

but because he made me feel good—
i became addicted to his presence
and smiled as wide as the earth when i could spot him
from miles away.

i was happy when it was time to go astray and do everything
i wanted him because he pleased my heart—
i wanted to follow the world, not Jesus because i didn't have
a relationship
with Him—i was lost in a world of my own—isolated from
Life.

i was addicted to his loud music and the rims on his car—
i knew my lover was on his way like romeo.
and the aroma in his car melted my heart with smiles--
his smell was unique—loud like the sweetest cologne in the
world.
and when he touched me, nothing else mattered.

i was addicted to his body and the sweet talks that led me
into captivity—
a dark wilderness filled with bedrooms that i was desperate
to jump into.
i was in love with his white covers, soft pillows, and my
precious, innocent body, riding on his train for years without
stops
because every ride gave me pleasure
like riding on a horse throughout the city of new orleans—
i was inexperienced, so i loved what made me feel good—
temporarily.

my flesh never said no because making love on top of an
unstable foundation was my addiction

i was on top of the world—of my own

my heart was weak and depressed because
i became addicted to sin and high off minutes of love with-
out a glove and words that sounded like love without a
heartbeat.

i was addicted to his hugs and text messages because
i thought it was real love.

i was addicted to hearing the same old song—
repeatedly
until enough was enough—
i desired a healthier life in Him than with him—my lover.

God removed the veil and stripped me down
until i was naked and on my knees praying for a change.

He renewed my mindset and motivated me to desire

righteousness over unrighteous living.

i was addicted to false love, but not anymore.
God opened my eyes and delivered me
from years of hurt and pain—
mentally, physically, and emotionally.

i'm healthy and free.

i'm no longer addicted to him, but now Him.

confidence

a phenomenal woman

you're a virtuous woman—
beautiful and sweet
and phenomenal
just like me.

you're the light amid every fight
and desire to live right.
you're a phenomenal woman
just like me.

no wonder your heart is filled with love
and compassion—you're a child of God
you're bold and courageous
and filled with joy
smiles
and gratitude because of His grace and mercy.
you embrace hugs
and love to make love.
you're a phenomenal woman
just like me.

you're a jewel and special treat to all the young ladies you
meet—
everyone loves your sassy attitude.
you're wise and disciplined
respectful
giving
and supportive to many as a neighbor should be.
and your significant other never worries if
you'll cheat
because he knows he can trust you
even while he's asleep.

you embrace your hands in the kitchen, on
paper,
and to all you feed—you're that kind of
woman—
phenomenal
just like me.

you're a god-fearing woman with imperfections

blemishes
and scars of life and traumas—
you're a blessing to all the young girls
in the world.

you're a praying woman who never gives up
even in the middle of storms and tragedy.
you're strong and phenomenal
just like me.

i love your zeal—you brighten the day of those who are
down and weak, lost, and lonely.

you inspire men and boys to make better choices
to live right
and to help the elderly.
your children respect you and praise God—
you're a great example and phenomenal woman
just like me.

patience is a part of your name, and everyone knows it.
you're selfless and obedient
and a dedicated follower of Jesus Christ.
you love to worship Him and glorify His holy name.
and when you rise you encourage others
to embrace their precious lives.

your actions speak louder than what you preach
and everyone thinks you're cool
down to earth
and funny.

ladies, you're more valuable than silver and gold
jewels
pearls
and diamonds.
you're blessed and highly favored
just like me.

we're phenomenal women.

celebrate

it's not my birthday, but i'm celebrating
because i'm happy and overjoyed
for life, health, and strength
and for the God, who lives in me.

i'm living to God be the glory.

i'm celebrating because i can face tomorrow—
the next day and the day after without doubt.
i sing with hope and faith in my heart.

my God knows i love to praise His name.
He's been good to me.

i'm celebrating life because God first loved me
before i loved me—oh, how i love the gift of the
world, the Great I Am.

i'm a special blessing so i love celebrating life.

i'm celebrating life because of Love,
i'm loved,
in love,
and a survivor.

i celebrate every day.

i'm a flower

i'm a flower waiting to exhale—to breathe
on this dark and unbelievable land—earth
but i can't because i'm malnourished—i'm weak and weiry.
my body is weak and i have no water, sunlight, and spiritual
food to grow—
to live and function in sync with God.
i'm just a flower—lifeless—i'm struggling with life
and i'm tired of being tired like almost miserable—i
feel isolated and like a prisoner in my own body—in the
ground—stuck as i watch the clock tick
tock for years, and i feel isolated from the world—
disconnected on purpose—but i don't know the answer or
maybe
i'll discover Him—one day before it's over.

i'm a flower and i'm hungry—i'm starving to live
in the One who created the world—
in the One who opens eyes and renews a weak and de-
pressed heart—
a worldly mindset.
i want to breathe and i need the Light—strength and pow-
er from God—i need grace and mercy or i'll parish in the
ground like many
who died before experiencing true life—life in Christ.

i'm a flower and i'm standing but i'm lacking nutrients—
the essentials to live beyond just breathing.
i'm holding on with hope and faith
to be blessed—to taste freedom—a renewed mindset—
life in the Creator—up above.

i'm a flower and i'm on my last…

but grace has fallen upon me and i'm happy—
i'm thankful and rejoice with open eyes.
i was weak but now i'm strong—in Christ.
i'm nourished by the word of God—i'm healthier than
ever—
praise God.

i was a flower without life—and near death
but God rescued me—He fed me and saved my life—
i shout—i rejoice with songs of thanksgiving—
to God be the glory.

the Son keeps me healthy.

my hair

i'm a beautiful, brown princess (a doll baby as many called
me)
with thick, long, pretty hair that bounced past my shoulders
when i walked, skipped, and ran as fast as i could
in neighborhoods and on the playground—
my hair went everywhere with me
because it was a part of me, and we loved each other like
best friends.
i loved when it flew in different directions, but
i didn't like sitting in a chair—i wasn't a fan of the comb—
i cried and jumped up and down as if there were ants in my
pants
but if you flew an airplane on the top of my head
you'd understand i was happy with my hair because it was
healthy.

i loved me and i loved the squares and circles that created
ponytails
twist, braids, and curls
in my beautiful, black hair.

i was a happy little girl.

her heart

her heart is the color of red wine and when she was younger, she knew that she was beautiful beyond "fine." she wasn't blind. she was disciplined and made sure my sisters and i were happy, healthy, and doing just fine. we embraced our quality time. Lord knows, sometimes, i wish i could turn back the hands of time like back to the future in doing a sudden rewind. but, if we did, there would be smiles and laughs, and a lot of crying while reminiscing about the years she gave her heart out to others who were unloving. yes, i'm telling the truth. i have no room to sit in a dark room while listening to outside noise and all that boom, boom, boom as we heard in my mother's room—an environment where we were surrounded by doom. i knew one day; we would soon bloom. my mother's heart is red like the color of wine and sweeter than the sweetest of all its colors of the same kind. she loved from a heart as precious, purposeful, and powerful as a dove. love was her only answer. she gave her heart out to everyone with lots of love, which came from way up, above. yes, her heart is the color of red like wine, raspberries, and sweet cherries. it's fruitful and sweet like blueberries. she always carried her heart; it was never buried but blessed by the best from a bag of imperfect, yet beautifully, blessed, and wonderfully made fruits like the human heart made by the hands that gave and gives us all chances to walk right, talk right, sing right, live right, and love right—by God and God alone. her precious, loving, and kind heart spilled and continues to spill over and into others like that of watching a rain fall of love from a human body with love given to the entire world. hers blessed and gave to others, unconditionally, and from the depths of her heart. no wonder her heart is healthy and filled with lots of love from way up above that spills and splashes over and

into the hearts of others, sisters and brothers, mothers, the
hopeless and homeless, and many others. it was her heart,
my mother's heartbeat that worked hard, watched us, loved
us and others, and stayed on her feet while my sisters and i
and father were sound asleep. she loved us like God Him-
self from above as we grew, gained, and glowed in such a
world of variety and uniqueness. but, her heart, oh, what a
magnificent and selfless heart she possessed—one that blos-
soms, enriches, enhances, and flourishes out to others like
the flowers in the garden that are planted and settled in the
most beautiful and eye-catching gardens on the planet. it's
nourished and seasoned with grace, and blessed by the Son
with lots of sun and favored with strength that releases pow-
er, purpose, patience, and the passion to love, in her every
heartbeat, a heart that pumped with confidence, courage, and
strength and one that was giving and operated its purpose
and functions with purpose on purpose and for a greater pur-
pose like the stunning and humongous universe, except her
heart— my mother's heart is one out of over a billion others
that was created and stationed in her body made of flesh
and blood, from dirt and mud, which produced and now
continues to expose her heart, a fruitful, caring, and loving
heart, one that's never sour—her heart—my mother's heart
was and is unique and extraordinary because she loved God,
herself, my sisters and i, father, and everyone else from the
heart. she gave from the heart, spoke from the heart, wrote
from the heart, shared from the heart, cared for others from
the heart, fed the able and disabled, and homeless from the
heart, gave advice and wisdom from the heart, sacrificed
her freedom for my sisters and i from the heart only to end
up imprisoned in a closed in, distanced, and secluded cell
where sometimes she fell as she climbed the hills to help
pay all the medical, dental, vision, phone, and utility bills
and provided for us and others at her best while getting little

rest. oh, no wonder i speak with words from the heart about how my mother is the best. she worked her buns off with little rest and sometimes went to bed with a lot on her chest as she worried about us and the rest. she loved from the heart and did her best. and as children she washed us with zest and dial as she sometimes walked miles with us with her big, contagious, beautiful smile. yes, she's God's child and never was she wild. she almost signed papers and filed, but because her heart runs like water flowing from the Nile, her heart stayed filled with a heart of love, inspired from way up above. she executed, walked, and talked like she did because she didn't know how not to love. she was a dedicated woman, wife, and mother, who exploded blood, sweat, and tears as she made sure we were fed, clothed, healthy, and nurtured the best way possible as she once worked one, two, and three jobs, until she signed a covenant contract with my father, who soon was led astray by drugs that placed a veil over his entire life—he was no longer the same, but lived to satisfy his flesh with a powerful destruction that nearly led him six feet under, after he suffered from a brain stroke—one that not only almost took his life, but also soul, but God rescued and recovered my father from a vegetation state to now a dedicated, committed, clean, and humble servant in the Lord. today, he walks with a renewed mindset by the Greatest love, who saved his life and gave him another chance to walk in a way to where now he knows no other way, except God and God alone. her heart answered the phone with the most precious tone. Love ruled and was and is her most powerful tool. her heart is the color of wine and never whines. her heart is still filled with a stadium of agape love, forgiveness, sympathy, and all the above, because God first loved us. yes, her heart executes with real love—love that's originated from our Heavenly Father from up above. she's virtuous woman with a heart filled with love. yes, my mother's heart is sweet, beautiful, and powerful like the finest art. Her heart.

her heart is my beautiful, special mother.

the journey

from creation to birth
my journey was like
the preparation of a cake
that took more than you'd ever imagine
like the length of time it took God to create and birth you
my creation was thoroughly planned
by the Creator
i was shaped and molded in my mother's womb
unconsciously baked to God's perfection
and delivered into this world
in a matter of hours
after it was time to execute
my God-given purpose
and the will of God
in a matter of minutes
after cooling off
and overcoming life
while spiritual darkness
hovered over my small
precious body
and settled in the blood
that was running warm
in my veins
until decades later
like experiencing two births
oh, what a journey
what a blessing
though painful
and beyond the *Nightmare on Elm Street*
i've walked talked

ate
fought, slept, cried, laughed, smiled
and endured
all on the journey of life.

embrace the journey.

i feel

i'm struggling with life like a human being
except i feel different—like i'm in a world all alone
so isolating myself feels better than connecting with the
world
because using my voice seems harder—it's more work
to use my mouthpiece—the one that has the power to en-
courage others and change lives.

i feel like an unusual child, different
from what i see on tv and in my neighborhood
i don't feel right because i'm unique
i'm not like everybody…i'm cool with that
but i feel disconnected
with the world and like maybe i don't belong here or just
that i'm different
which is probably not a bad thing—it's good
but sometimes i feel like the loneliest person on the planet.
i feel no one hears me
no one cares and doesn't wanna be my friend.
wasn't i created by the same God who created you?
i'm to the point where i feel i'm certain i'm not alone
so, holla if ya hear me—if you're bold enough to rise and
share
your feelings on the page to help somebody else
to help a stranger, loved one
or even, to encourage yourself—like don't we all need en-
couragement
every now and then or if we feel this way?
i do
because i feel how many others do—different
but in a good way
in a positive way that lets me stand out
in a way that now makes me feel better
confident

stronger than ever.

i feel better because i'm wiser
and more confident than i was growing up
and even now.

i feel you because i've walked in your shoes (in a different
size)
i've looked in that mirror and felt all alone
like hello, is anybody in here…
i've felt disconnected and like i was the strangest
and weirdest person on the earth.

i feel better than good.

i feel human because i am
and i'm certain because it's just a feeling
that all who were created by God
have felt the same.

i'm thankful and appreciative.
i'm okay because my eyes are open
thank God—the One who created me to be human
to have feelings—to feel and express my heart
without limits—an experience worth the experience.

i feel like you but not like what you're thinking.

i will always feel because i'm supposed to—
i'm a human being
a woman with a heart, so i feel you.

permit yourself to feel.

.

letting go

i'm restless and i know why.
i just lost my dam job and it's bothering me.
i can't sleep because my mind is playing tricks on me.
i'm tossing in bed like a cranky newborn
because my circumstance is overpowering my faith.
i feel confused but not lost because i know i'm saved.
i'm a child of God with a thorn in my flesh
and it hurts but not bad enough for me to overcome it.
my flesh is fighting with the world but i know there is hope.

a lot is on my mind
i'm ready to let go and let God take over my life
and i'm serious because i'm tired of struggling
in this skin like my neighbor.
i'm tired of going back and forth, fighting in the ring
with the Satan and my heart.
i know something is about to happen
but i don't know when nor do you except my Father.
i hope it's soon though because i'm ready to live.
i'm ready for change, for a new chapter.
the one i'm in feels like hell.
i'm unhappy and unsatisfied.
change is about to happen, and Lord knows i'm ready.
i feel it in my bones and in my heart.
i wanna breathe like a noisy caged bird who wants freedom.
but i don't know what to do
until my heart unclogs words from my heart
in a space where i'm certain others would be inspired.
my heart is releasing words on my phone like every breathe
i take
at the pace of my heart.
i'm writing how i feel because i know my words have pow-

er.
and i feel good like never before.
after writing for hours past midnight
i feel like i'm on top of the world.
i feel better but i know this journey of healing is going to
take time
like overcoming trauma.

my heart is finally smiling.
i'm satisfied, pleased with what God revealed to me.
my heart is free but not perfect.
i'm healthier than my last chapter.
i'm thankful because my heart and calling are one.
i welcomed my passion in my life with open arms
and it feels good.
letting go of the truth
thoughts
feelings
hurt
embarrassment
pain
and joy
is what i desired to do all the while long.
i feel fulfilled.

i feel good.

worth

i'm worth more than your wildest dreams—
far greater than you'd ever imagine.
i was created with value
by mighty hands
and blessed to do amazing things.
i was born on purpose to embrace
all that i am
to walk by faith
and to move with confidence.
i was designed to reach for the stars
to succeed and be all that God created
you and i to be.
my life is full of grace, love, and mercy.
no wonder my heart is beating and i'm free.
my life is priceless.
money doesn't define me.
my life is worth more than nickels and dimes
quarters
pennies
and paper.

your education doesn't label you
and your appearance doesn't identify you.

your purpose is far greater than your failures
and everything you have—inside and out
in front of you.

you're worth more than words
the good and the bad—the ones that make you feel uncomfortable
embarrassed

ugly
and like a piece of trash as if you aren't human.

you're worth more than silver and gold and diamonds.
you're like a jewel—a special blessing from above.
no matter who you are, you're worth it
so black out
what you look like.
and what you're wearing
you're worth more than you'd ever imagine.

you are precious.

you are somebody. you're different. you stand out.

nobody

in the midst of life like the unexpectedness that passes
across the earth,
when tomorrow looks hopeless and you feel all alone
there's nobody like Jesus—like our Lord and Savior
the One, who's there in the chaos and trials and tribulations
of life
when nothing seems to make sense
and when everything seems dark and confused.
there's nobody who can bless you, protect and rescue
like Jesus, the Son of God, who suffered beyond your imag-
ination.
there's nobody who gives grace like our Father
whose Son also gives power to humanity.
there's nobody who can do it like the Lord—
the One and only who sustains life
comforts hearts
provides like no one else
and wakes us up in our right mind.

there's nobody like the Lord who can turn someone's
crooked life straight and bless the poor with wisdom
like no other and by no other except through the Lord.
He turned my life around and transformed my mindset.

there's nobody like Jesus—the One who gives peace
and gave me a new song to sing—a song of gratitude
and appreciation.
He continues to renew my mindset
and nourish my soul.
there's nobody like Jesus.

there's nobody like my best friend, Jesus.

in Him

gazing into a microscope seems strange
but it's now making total sense like the solution of
getting a job to earn a living or maybe the other way
around...
i see all my confusion mixed
like staring at a blender with every fruit on the planet
united for one special purpose.

like an animal on the hunt in Him i found everything that i
wasn't seeking
i found hope, faith, and love—unlike what i searched for
on my journey of life
like a person who finds Life in the storm.

if you're looking for something
look no further because He's alive and rules the world.
He's the truth, way, and life.
in the Lord we live like a healthy person with spiritual vi-
sion
in Jesus Christ i am living.

no wonder i have joy in my heart
i am free in Him.

in Jesus we find justice, receive second chances
like a teacher gives to a student on a test of life.
in Christ there is hope because Hope is alive.

i'm living in Him.

i surrendered my life to Him.

rise

ladies and gentlemen
rise
when you trip and fall
stumble over obstacles
and struggle with life.

when you fail
stand up and be strong with the power God has given you.

be brave like our ancestors and persevere with your
remarkable resilience
when life breaks you—
never let it crush you.

pray in your storms and keep the hope.
you're strong and have the power to overcome life
despite spiritual warfare.
keep striving to overcome this internal fight.
God will turn your lemons into lemonade
He'll turn your pain into passion
and bless you to bless others
like hard, fighting soldiers and single mothers.
so be comforted
and rejoice with faith
even when unexpectedness comes your way.
everything will be okay.
embrace the freckles and dimples on your face
and be happy with your tattoos on areas where many have
turned their backs on you.
i love it when i see *In God, We Trust*
along with painted scars on arms that read
Grace & Mercy.

so, ladies and gentlemen
rise
be wise
and be cautious with your eyes.
turn right before left
and listen with your ears.
be motivated when you're happy and weak.
desire to teach the young.
you're bold.
you have the power to inspire the old.
be empowered to climb these difficult mountains
and hills of hope
opportunity
freedom
and equality.
ladies and gentlemen
rise
and smile.
teach others the right way to live
spread the Word
and pray for lives.
you're the light of the world.
so, stand out because you're outstanding.
you can do it.
you will make it.
oh, yes
you can and you will.
rise.

let's rise with love and walk in harmony.

a star

dear me,

where are you?
you're a star but i don't see you.
are you hiding somewhere on this earth?
if so, why? you're beautiful and special
so, shine, or else you'll continue looking like the world.
you were created and brought into this world to stand out,
to shine your light amongst all men and women
but you haven't—you're wasting your precious life away.
time is running out, so shine with confidence—you're it—
you're one of a kind and built to do so.

you were designed to be the light that shines in chaos and
crises
and the star that inspires others to turn to Jesus Christ
but where are you?

here i am
i'm out standing where i stood all along—
i was here for years, but i lived in darkness
and lacked confidence and self-esteem to just shine and be
me—
the person God created me to be—a star.

i'm no longer in darkness.

i'm a bright star.

this little light of mine will forever shine.

i'm shining, to God be the glory.

beyond the walls

like the rooster that crows from miles away
with a voice so loud, bold, and confident
let us break our generational curses.
let us break the walls of silence with speechless voices
in telling truths to help others along the way
to make the right choices
not to get divorces, but to pray and live on fire with
faith to encourage inspire, and motivate others.
to stick in and stick out their hands.
to give others a chance
and with hearts minus the negative remarks.
to climb the mountains where everyone has
and will sin but to shout before us to know
that there is hope
not on the corner watching your brother sell
dope.
there's always light at the beginning, middle, and end of the
tunnel
with all who were blessed with voices to shine
even amid our secret grinds
we can't rewind
but we can look to the hills that lie in front of us
and press the start button so we can begin our
walk and talk
and try again as we press forward
to step in and stand in our purpose
to be that light when it's dark
to be that light when the switch has been burned
awaiting to turn
to be that light when everyone ignores and closes the
doors
to be that light when everyone is against the chores
of living obedient and disciplined lives
praising, glorifying, and honoring God.

to be that light in front of and behind closed doors
and to be that light beyond the walls where you see your
flaws.
let us shine
not just when fine dining
drinking the tastiest wine.
many are on the streets crying
trying to stop buying
and attending late night parties
where many are praying to take life one day at a time
living on Skit Row without a dime.
many are still crying and sleeping out on the roads dying
they're trying
while many are using their two senses so they can jump
over the fence of hell denial, discrimination, affliction,
and a whole lot of addiction
with tears of joy hidden
but some realize flying without ever sharing their stories
will be boring
so, speak up and speak out all your truths without lying
beyond the walls where everyone is called to love
not to wear gloves
just to knock down and shove
but to glow in the streets of darkness and behind the scenes
where no one sees the true hearts that are bitter with tart
let's embark beyond the world of walls
that continue to keep our mouths closed, hearts hidden, and
fire from burning coals of love, hope, faith, trust, forgive-
ness, peace, humility, support, care, empathy, and drive to
defeat our greatest enemy.
let's stand up and stand out
speak up and speak out
beyond the walls of insecurities, shame, guilt, sadness, an-
ger, and hate without a debate
beyond the walls.

listen to hearts.

glow

you glow
like the magnificent sunrise
as bright as the streetlights
where you stood on the corner and watched many fights
and saw smoke that made you choke
while you sipped on a coke.
so, honey, rise.
overlook the unloving names
embrace these words
just because you went from door to door seeking a show
with your red ribbon bow
short skirt the color of dirt
and shirt
you will one day, rise
with your black and white skin
and brown chin
and show all men and women
what it means to truly glow
with your puffy afro.
have faith that you will
gain and grow.
the Lord knows
that one day
you will grow big, bold, and old
and continue to glow.

you're already special.

you're a winner

look up, dear
you're a winner
so, rise
and never give up.
stand up
no matter what you face
we're all on this unpredictable race
yes
stay focused
and never look back
stay on track.
breathe
and know that every little thing
will be alright.
open your eyes
and rise
and never lose hope.
sit up and listen up
and keep your eyes on the finish line.
you'll succeed.
yes
rise
and have faith.
never doubt
but be certain.
this is what life is all about.
so, stand up
with confidence and determination
move forward
with the strength God created you with
you're stronger than you think
and more powerful than your greatest fear
so, don't worry

smile and be thankful
you're blessed
and highly favored.

you're a winner.

my first love-music

the sound of music

it's black and silver
wooden
and heavy.
it has twenty-four keys and sounds like the human voice—
my voice.

my clarinet is not any instrument
or something that doesn't produce music.
it's a musical instrument.

i'm young and curious by this new language—music
and gazing at five lines and four spaces excites my precious
little heart—it's apart of my life, so what can i say?

it's amazing looking at awkward symbols and signs
like the treble clef sign,
fraction-like symbols that represented meters,
and lowercased letters that identify as key signatures.

playing music is like riding the bike for the first time
and speaking another language—it's a process that takes time.
i had to start with the basics
like a builder starting from the foundation.
music soothes the mind and heals--
it encourages others and continues to motivate my spirit.

however, the black notes never made sense to my heart—
it was chicken scratch
in the eyes of an adolescent
until i began to comprehend my gift
and embrace the process of learning
music.

i enjoy reading from left to right—
day and night and expressing my heart.

no wonder music is my passion—
when i played, every note represented my thoughts and feel-
ings.

the clarinet is my second voice.
i adore what exits through the bell
i am comforted and uplifted
in times of need and i enjoy watching my fingers press down
on keys
over finger holes that produce beautiful sounds.

sometimes i play loud and soft and enjoy moving my fingers
around the clarinet,
over the upper and lower sections,
across the bridge,
and near the barrel
like the experience of embracing my body with freedom.

playing music is a shield—
an environment i feel protected.
i feel apart of something—deeply connected like a husband
and a wife.

i'm inspired to let go when i perform on the clarinet, but
there's more
i need to say that i'm struggling with…

i carry it everywhere and i'm always moved to express my-
self.
i persevered in times of darkness
and prayed at dawn
and sunset.
i never gave up on my goals
i stood strong like a tree that's planted in the ground

and soared with wings like an eagle.

i overcame life
and played my heart out.
however, my heart was weak.
deep, down, inside
my heart was suffering.

my calling needed me more than my dream.

i enjoyed creating music
like painting on a wall.
music will forever touch my heart
and rests in my soul.

i will always embrace the sound of music.

my first love will never leave my heart.

the human roar

like a lion that stands in the middle of life and roars on pur-
pose and with purpose
the human heart roars every second, every day, and every
hour
as the earth spins with purpose
with a sounding roar of confusion and doubt
and clueless to what life is all about
only because the human roar yearns to release
as it tries to seek the Lord.
it continues to roar with scars
as it walks imprisoned in a body made from dust
we're still born and blessed to soar
and gain so much more
with a deep and intimate relationship with the Source
if only we sat down, and all made the right choice to follow
His voice
you'd understand that the human roar has to say so much
more
with so much on one's chest to get up and get out
to hurry up and invest in a clutter of mess
while our young ones stand and watch their fathers get shot
down, beat down, imprisoned, chained, and carried away
with so much to say
yet many of them get sent away while the innocent rest ev-
ery day.
the human roar is sometimes hidden behind a vest
only to lose like playing chess
but listen up, we were born to roar but soar through every
unexpected and
unpleasant door, so don't ignore
we all have chores to stand up and stand tall against every
evil wall

with the motivation and desire to be the change
like Paul, so brothers, stand up tall and stay fo-
cused so you don't fall
remember, we're all climbing this hill and will
get ill
but that doesn't mean chill
keep striving and let God do the driving.
make the best out of every day
as you lift your eyes to the hills and pray with hope, faith,
and confidence. i hear you through the chaos and crisis, and
unbearable agony
of life. embrace the roar
until there's nothing left of you except memories of your
story
untold songs of your life and recordings that were hidden in
your heart.
release.

a roar happens before your deliverance.

freedom

honey, fly

like birds that fly
up in the sky
you too were born to crawl, climb,
and fly
so, release your passion
without fear.
you have more than what it takes
to rise
and overcome the obstacles of life.
you were created with power.

like the eagles that fly
up in the sky
you too were born to crawl, climb,
and fly
with your visible voice.
so, persevere
strive
and look beyond the difficult hills.
stand up and believe in yourself.
you're an overcomer.

like butterflies that fly
beyond the trees in the garden
you too were born to crawl, climb,
and fly
with strength in your heart.
you're blessed by a powerful God,
so be courageous and soar.

like doves that fly
up to the sky

you too were born to crawl, climb,
and fly
so, don't be shy
be bold before you grow old.
you weren't born to perish
but to live.

like birds that fly
up to the sky
you too were born to crawl, climb,
and fly,
to slip and fall
lose and win
so, never give up.
you're strong on the outside and within.
you'll make it over the hurdles of life.
you will win.
honey, fly.

have faith and fly.

i'm free

as i lift my head to the sky
i rise with open eyes
like a beautiful butterfly who flies.

i stand tall with confidence
because better days are here
and better days are coming.

no wonder my faith is stronger than the wind
and my heart rejoices in my calling.

here, i rise like a soldier
in Christ.
i'm blessed because i'm living—i'm standing on my two
feet
with appreciation and humility.
grace made a way out of no way.

i'm touched like a proud Father
and excited like a mother expecting...
because i'm free.
and this i know.
the Word tells me so—i'm certain without a doubt.
i'm free.
i can breathe
because i'm living.
i can see because the veil was
removed
to God be the glory.
yes
this is my true story.
it's unplugged

raw
and real
without edits or revisions.
my flaws and imperfections
can never be erased like the scars of my life
because my destiny was planned
by an awesome God.
after so many years
i can smile without hiding behind my gift.
i love my voice
my heart
and my hands.
i burst in joy
with thanksgiving for grace and mercy.
i stand erect with my shoulders relaxed
in my right mind
and with it focused on Jesus.
i'm thankful because
my heart is in sync with Christ.
i can finally see.
i hear my heartbeat.
to God be the glory.
i'm free, at last.
thank God, Almighty.
i'm free.

i can finally breathe.

A bonus

To

You

From

My

Heart

i'm happy, and i know it

because my heart is healthy

it's stronger than ever

like my mind

i'm happy, and i know it.

i'm imperfect, and that's okay

i'm free

i feel good

in the voice of James Brown.

i'm happy, and i know it

not because you see me smile

i'm happy, and i know it

my heart and mind

agree

like two lovers shaking their heads

we're inseparable

i'm refreshed

My God renewed my mind

like a lamp plugged into an outlet

with power

i'm finally smiling

i love what's in the mirror

my smile is beautiful.

i'm happy, and i know it

but it feels kind of weird

like walking into a new life

with a transformed mindset

when i stretch my cheeks

but it feels good to finally say cheese

with confidence

in this skin

after so many years

like losing over a hundred pounds

and adjusting to your new size.

i'm happy, and i know it without looking

in the mirror for confirmation

i love myself, and i love you, too.

i'm happy and i know it.

express yourself with confidence.

Other books by Kala Jordan-Lindsey

The Most Powerful Quotes to Enhance Your Life: Inspirational and Motivational Quotations to Strengthen Your Mental, Physical, and Spiritual Health

when you rise: Book 2, 2ⁿᵈ Edition

when you rise: Book 2

when you rise: Book 1, 2ⁿᵈ Edition

when you rise: Book 1

words from the heart: 1ˢᵗ Edition

Run Your Business in Ten Essentials for 365 Days and Beyond

If you enjoyed reading this book, including the first edition, please leave a comment on Amazon. I read every review, and your feedback helps new readers discover my books. Thank you. God bless.

Acknowledgements

To my Heavenly Father,

Thank you for giving me the confidence to release my heart in a space where others would be inspired and blessed.

To my family and friends,

Thank you for your love, support, and prayers since the beginning of my new chapter. I love you beyond the stars.

To my publishing team,

Thank you for your time, gift, and professionalism.

To my readers,

Thank you for being a part of my journey. I hope you find these words of hope, inspiration, and healing light in your darkness to help you overcome life one day at a time.

About the Author

Kala Jordan-Lindsey is an American writer and poet known for her love and passion on the page. She writes nonfiction, fiction, children's books, memoirs, poetry and prose, self-help books, romance, faith-based books, and more. Kala was born and raised in Delray Beach, Florida, and currently resides in Miami, Florida, with her husband and their beautiful daughter.

When she is not writing, Kala enjoys relaxing, reading, listening to music, spending time with her family and talking with friends, cooking healthy meals, exercising, dancing, quiet time, traveling, Friday date nights, helping others on their self-publishing journey, and living life to the fullest.

You can chat with Kala on Facebook, LinkedIn, or Instagram, or browse her website at www.kalajordanlindsey.com, and sign up to receive her monthly newsletters and inspirational messages.

Ingram Content Group UK Ltd.
Milton Keynes UK
UKHW020844130423
420096UK00006B/40